Believe

Believe

A Life Touched by Miracles

Gaby Pineda

Published by Tablo

Copyright © Gaby Pineda 2023.
Published in 2023 by Tablo Publishing.

All rights reserved.

This book or any portion thereof may not be reproduced or used in any manner whatsoever without the express written permission of the author except for the use of brief quotations in a book review.

Publisher and wholesale enquiries: orders@tablo.io

20 21 22 23 LSC 10 9 8 7 6 5 4 3 2 1

Table of Contents

Believe	1
Acknowledgements and Gratitude	2
Believe	5
The Beginning	7
A Unique Duck	11
The First Miracle	21
The Miracle of The Sacred Heart	27
My First Sensei	34
The Miracle of DNA Memories	45
My Awareness of Past Life Memories	47
Prima Ballerina	52
A Connection to Horses	55
A Connection to The Ocean	62
The Starseed Connection	65
French Warrior	68
Miracles In the Jungle	76
The Miracle of Eternal Life	98
The Miracle of Communication	109
The Miracle of Awareness and Manifestation	116
The Miracle of Forgiveness	127
The Miracle of Conception	133
The Miracle of Unconditional Love	138
The Miracle of Divine Intervention	145
The Miracle of Divine Protection	150
The Miracle of Self-Healing	153

The Miracle of Spirit's Love	**163**
The Miracle of a Mother's Love	**166**
The Miracle of a Fallen Hero	**169**
The Miracle of Your Superpowers	**177**
Claircognizance	**179**
Clairolfaction	**184**
Clairgustance	**185**
Clairsentience	**188**
Astral Projection	**190**
Telephathy	**192**
Pre-cognition or Clairvoyance	**193**
Psychokinesis or Telekinesis	**197**
Energy Medicine	**202**
Medical Intuition	**204**
Automatic Writing/Drawing	**206**
Seeing and Reading Auras	**207**
Clearing Energy Fields and Helping Spirits Cross Over	**209**
The Miracle of 'Conviction'	**217**
The Miracle of Energy Healing Technology	**222**
The Miracle That Healed Jesus	**227**
The Power of Limiting Beliefs	**233**
The Miracle of Self-Love	**237**
The Miracle of Connection	**249**
Closing Remarks	**252**
About the Author	**254**

Believe

A Life Touched by Miracles

By Gaby Pineda

Acknowledgements and Gratitude

I am grateful for Source energy, that which we are all made from and are part of, for the guidance on writing this book.

Thank you to my guardian angels (star beings, Ascended Masters and Archangels, especially, Archangel Michael, and spirit guides (Aunt Leonor, Mom, Dad, Grandma Minnie, Angelo, Abuelo, Tio Javo, Tacha, my unborn children, Christian Patrick and Alexandra Isabella, as well as my furry kids, Nikki and Coco in spirit) for your constant guidance and unconditional love.

Thank you to my Zen cat, Luna, and my angelic dog, Pachis, for showing me how to chill and for your unconditional love.

A special thanks to Grandma Minnie for believing in me. I feel your love every day. You shine through me and I shine through you.

My appreciation goes out to my friends and family for your support.

Thank you to Carol McBride, my university roommate and proofreader, who gave the final polish to my writing. God bless your patience.

I am grateful for my beta readers, Andrew Kirkwood, Joseph De Melo and Wendy Parfrey, for taking the time out of your busy schedules to read this book and give me your honest feedback from the reader's perspective, which was instrumental in making this book what it is today.

Andrew Kirkwood, a special thanks to you for offering to beta read my book from a professional writer's viewpoint.

A few years back, your offer may have made me feel vulnerable because let's face it, no one likes their work being critiqued, but no insecurities came up when you offered. I just knew it was a "Yes, please…and thank you."

Thank you for your kind words, generosity, expert suggestions and honest feedback.

Never did I imagine what it would lead to, but I am forever grateful.

This was yet another validation from Source to be in the flow of things.

My gratitude goes out to Tiomi at Blair Ann Embrace Photography Studio for proving that you can make anyone look like a superstar and feel as powerful as they are.

Your one-stop magical transformation team (styling, hair, and make-up) combined with your deep understanding of your subject's needs, personality and essence make you exceptional.

However, your direction, photographic skill and ability to capture inner beauty and empowerment through a lens were the keys to achieving the front cover of this and future books.

Many thanks to my social media team, Antonio and Vanessa Urdaneta at Hutbee.com, who make my life so much easier.

Thank you for understanding the humanity of business, your flexibility and compassion. It is a pleasure working with you.

I am grateful for the clients who put your trust in me to deliver the messages from your loved ones and for allowing me into your energetic field.

Thank you to the spirits who choose me as your interpreter to relay messages of love, hope, compassion and forgiveness for your loved ones.

My appreciation goes out to Jason Troy, one of my spiritual advisors, for putting me on the path of becoming a professional reader.

My gratitude goes to Shadia and Mira for giving me the opportunity to join such a wonderful group of professional readers.

Thank you Sindy, Judy, Luc, Blaize, Dave, Carol, Grace, Danny, Kristina, Ennio, Angelo, Lynda, Paul, Ruben, Mike, Darren, Darun, Christina, Mandy, Linda, Joanne, Polina, Aaron, Toni, Frances, Ydania, Ed, for your friendship, thoughtfulness and generosity.

Thank you to Ally, Dr. H, Jahmall and Felix for being part of my recovery team.

Thank you to my colleagues in the spiritual community for your support and encouragement, especially Jordanna and Ellen for being so kind to me from day one. Also Bob & Theresa, Maddy, Charlotte, Susan, Darren, Jesse, Klaudija, Nicole, Marika, Dorota, Emma (R.I.P.), Rorey Moon, Gina, Richard, Teressa, Salim, Holy, Mark, Tammy, and Krissy.

Thank you to all the people who haven't supported me because you were there to test my faith and trust.

Thank you to Colette Baron-Reid for encouraging me to start writing my life story over 30 years ago.

I remember the first thing you said to me when I walked into your office for the very first time, "What are you doing here if you're more psychic than I am?"

Then you told me that the book I was putting together in little pieces of scrap paper would be made into a movie.

I have to admit that I thought you were out of your mind at the time, but I followed your suggestions and here we are today.

I've always been a writer, I just didn't realize it would become my biggest passion, creative outlet and connection to Source.

To my husband, Gabriel, thank you for never giving up. Te amo.

My heart beats happier and wider thanks to your contributions.

Thank you for being in my life.

With love and gratitude,

Gaby

Believe

Many years ago, my grandmother gave me a bookmark.

I've kept it ever since because it symbolizes her strength,
power and faith in God,
that I would one day surrender consciously to.

The bookmark has one simple word, "Believe".

She was the inspiration for this book and its title.

My hope for you in reading these stories is that you reflect on
just how much of a miracle you are, and that you too,
can step into your Divine essence and powers.

You are Source energy.

Namaste,
(The Divine in me honors the Divine in you)

Gaby Pineda

"Knock, and he'll open the door,
Vanish, and He'll make you shine like the sun.
Fall, and He'll raise you to the heavens.
Become nothing, and He'll turn you into everything."
-Rumi-

The Beginning

"Pay attention to the signs," Grandma Minnie used to say to me. "God is always giving us signs to guide us along our path. The problem is, most people don't pay attention. Believe in the power of God."

Religion, as defined by Dictionary.com, is:

"A set of beliefs concerning the cause, nature and purpose of the universe, especially when considered as the creation of a super human agency or agencies, usually involving devotional and ritual observances, and often containing a moral code governing the conduct of human affairs."

Spirituality is defined as, "of or relating to the spirit or soul, as distinguished from the physical nature: *a spiritual approach to life.*"

I've never been religious; however, I've always been spiritual, even before I knew what spirituality was.

I was pleasantly surprised after reading a book by the Dalai Lama, because it was the first time a religious leader said, "If you like Buddhism, take what you like out of it and incorporate it into your belief systems, but do not convert."

What?

Every other religion emphasized conversion, but not Buddhism. So, that's what I did. I took what I liked and left the rest behind.

That little book changed my life.

This book is about my experiences growing up as an empath with several 'clairs' (a technical term used to define extra-sensory abilities, such as psychic or mediumship abilities), my spiritual development, as well as my resistance and eventual acceptance of my path.

Becoming a full-time professional 'reader' was far from straightforward for me. I fought it almost every step of the way.

After all, I had a university education and post-grad diplomas. I wasn't about to become a 'fortune teller' anytime soon.

I'd also changed careers after spending fifteen years in the corporate world. So, changing careers once again ten years later wasn't on my radar.

The typical doubts and questions that often accompany such radical decisions were very much part of my thought patterns.

A professional career as a psychic medium simply wasn't something I'd ever considered, but Jack, my tough-love spiritual mentor, kept repeating the same message, "Whether you do it now or at 90, this is your path. Why are you resisting so much?"

The truth is, I had no idea at the time. Now I know it was nothing other than fear of failure, disappointing others, not being good enough, and self-judgement.

Once I had a clear understanding of where those fears stemmed from, I began to open up more to the idea of accepting myself unconditionally, until I finally surrendered.

I tested Source by saying, "If I'm meant to do this for a living from now on, then bring the right opportunities to me."

The next day, I reached out to a woman who was one of the readers at a psychic fair to ask her what her experience had been on the road. She turned out to be one of the show organizers.

The rest is history.

Another thing I've learned is that we don't always choose our path. The path chooses us, and no matter how much we fight it, we'll eventually end up on it, if that is what we're meant to be doing.

The sooner we surrender to our path, the faster the internal conflict ends.

I lost friends and family along the way, but I see that as no different than an exfoliation; shedding that which, or those whom, we're no longer in resonance with.

Although I've never been religious, I've always been aware of my close relationship with God.

I had a hard time fitting in as a kid. At the age of three, I told my Grandmother Minnie that God and I had a special relationship, and I didn't have to go to church to be close to God because God was inside of me. I hadn't been told that by anyone, I just knew it.

However, I have to admit that much like with other interpersonal relationships, there was a time in my life when I told God our relationship was over.

I can imagine the 'laughing out loud' emoji wave that my statement created in the Field.

My brother Andrew, who was two years older than me and whom I considered my protector and friend, experienced what was referred to as a nervous breakdown in early 1982.

At the young age of 14, my perspective was that if the all-mighty and powerful God couldn't heal my brother Andrew's mind, then there would be no further conversations between God and me.

I had offered my life in exchange for my brother's healing from the turmoil he was experiencing with schizophrenia, but I was still alive months later; and my brother was still sick.

So, I stopped talking to God. I stopped believing, trusting and paying attention to signs.

If 'He' wouldn't make my brother better in exchange for my life, then what good was 'He'?

I thought it was a worthy exchange, but at that time in my life, I failed to understand the grander view, soul contracts, soul choices, individual paths, and letting go of the need to try to control others' paths.

Each of us is a soul who chose to incarnate into a human 'sleeve', and each of us has a path to live in the human experience we selected, much like playing a virtual reality game in a holographic reality.

This concept took me years to become aware of, understand and accept.

Jack, one of my spiritual counsellors, whom I mention often throughout this book, said, "Do you want to know why you chose this life?"

"Please enlighten me because I must've been stoned and drunk when I chose my mission."

"Because no one else would take it, and since you've always been kick-ass brave and loved challenges, you said, 'I'll do it!'"

The following stories depict the miracles which have proven to me time and time again, not only that God exists, but that the God within each of us is indeed, mighty.

More importantly, because God is inside each of us, we are Source energy. We are sacred, and there's always a higher plan for us.

I've let go of many beliefs taught to me in the Catholic religion, including God having a 'gender', which just happened to be male, that God is a punishing entity that must be feared, and that forgiveness is necessary in order to be allowed past the Pearly Gates.

I honor the Catholic values that I grew up with, but listen to and trust the messages that Source gives me every day.

Some of you will have experienced similar stories. Some of you won't believe a word I say. Either way is OK.

My intention is not to convince anyone of anything.

I'm simply sharing my personal stories from the perspective of a soul living a human experience.

Your experience is unique too.

If reading this book helps you believe, understand, or connect with your Divine essence, then it was worth writing.

If not, then perhaps you'll find it entertaining.

Also, I've changed the names of the people involved and other specific details in order to protect their privacy.

Lastly, I end each chapter with a moment for reflection, to encourage you to look into your own life and experiences in hopes that you acknowledge some of the miracles in your life.

A Unique Duck

I've always been different, even at birth.

My father, Lalo, often complained that I was born in a public hospital in Mexico City in the midst of what he referred to as, "one of the worst rain storms in history."

He was a bit of a drama king when it came to that story.

I'm not sure how much worse it could've been, considering that the rainy season in Mexico City is about as bad as I've ever seen.

It rains every day as if waterfalls were placed above the city. Wearing rain boots and carrying a sturdy umbrella are a requirement because floods throughout the city are just part of everyday life.

In July 1968, my mother was panting her way to a hospital in the back of a yellow VW Beetle.

I was inside her trying to make my entrance into the world, but the roads were flooded and traffic was stopped.

The scene was biblical, as rain came down from the heavens with blackened skies and rattling thunder that scared even the strongest souls.

Umbrellas didn't stand a chance against the wrath of winds that moved everything in their way.

The taxi driver was unable to get my mother to the hospital, but was kind enough to drop her off at the nearest clinic.

"You were born in candlelight!" my father recalled with disgust, as if candlelight was degrading.

"I don't think it was a coincidence, I love dim lighting."

My father had a hard time letting go of the past and talked about my mother till the day he died.

I felt terrible for my stepmother, Bruna, whenever he brought up my mother in front of her.

"Dad, it's been forty years since your divorce. Please stop talking about my mother as if it were yesterday. Get over it."

I didn't enjoy having to remind him. It was uncomfortable, even for me.

"There were streaks of dirt on the walls and the hallways wreaked of anesthetic!"

"Well, you know me. I had to come into this world in a unique way."

My maternal grandmother, Angela, commented during her second visit to Canada in twenty years, "Even at the age of three, you spoke like a hundred-year-old woman. You always had your head on straight. I don't understand why your mother strayed so far."

I knew I wasn't like other children. As a child, I was dreadfully bashful. I couldn't even change in front of other girls, so I went into bathroom stalls or waited till everyone had left the changeroom before putting on my bathing suit or gym clothes.

The private Catholic school I attended in Mexico City didn't help matters, with their strict ways and sometimes ruthless disciplinary methods, which reinforced the fears that I lived with every day at my maternal grandparents' home.

To add to this, I didn't understand any 'dirty' jokes my friends made at school until I was in high school.

Sad, but true.

Sure, I laughed at the jokes, but had no idea what I was laughing at. I just didn't want to be judged as 'stupid' for not knowing what they meant.

I've always been a walking lie detector, but it was hard for me to call "bullshit!" whenever someone lied to me. Though as an adult, I often fantasized about saying it, followed by an apology for my inability to hold back due to a speech disorder.

Instead, I tried to convince myself that I was being 'paranoid', only to prove to myself later on that I'd been right all along.

Children my own age weren't interesting to me, but adults and adult conversations were.

I preferred spending time alone with my dolls. I suppose it was because I could control all aspects of the game. It was safer than interacting with others.

Solitude has always been my friend. I feel cozy and warm when I'm in my own company.

'Seeing' events before they happened, whether in my dreams or as holographic movies in front of me, really scared me and I had no idea how to stop the visions.

Anxiety was also a friend, although an unwanted one. I was a worrywart and felt a tremendous sense of responsibility, especially when I saw the adults around me behave in ways they shouldn't.

My stomach felt like it was being squeezed, and the contents would propel in every direction anytime I 'felt' things being off.

Now I understand why I suffered as a child from chronic bronchitis, intestinal and ear infections. Worry made me hold my breath, lowered my immune system, affected my heart chakra and the areas where most of my stress collected – my stomach and lungs.

I got ear infections because I didn't want to hear the words I heard around me – my maternal grandparents' abusive remarks, my father's insults towards my mother, and my uncles' abusive remarks towards Grandma Minnie, my paternal grandmother.

I worried about everyone and everything, feeling responsible for their wellbeing and safety.

My need to 'rescue' others was satisfied by bringing home stray dogs and other animals, which drove my mother crazy because on two occasions, the dogs had scabies and I had to be quarantined.

I learned my lesson after the second incident, but suffered in silence at my inability to offer them shelter from the uncertainty of the streets.

Unconsciously, I connected with their feelings of abandonment and wanted to make it better.

Grandma Minnie was my best friend, protector and perfect companion.

She encouraged me to play games which allowed my creativity and entrepreneurial skills to shine.

We would go into her office, just off the main entrance to her house, and take on our avatars, "Which would you like to be today, store owner or teacher?"

She left it up to me to be the leader or supporting player in the game.

Most times I chose to be the protagonist. Unless I needed to learn something and then I chose to be the client or student.

She encouraged me to apply my math skills by keeping tabs on my sales and outstanding balances in customer accounts, which improved my sales and communication skills.

Not bad for a woman who never went to school and taught herself to read and write. She was one of the most educated people I've ever had the pleasure of knowing.

Grandma Minnie was born in one of the world's few and unique matriarchal societies in the world: Juchitán, Oaxaca, Mexico.

Her mother was indigenous, but not her father. She never met him, but her looks were a testament to that.

Grandma Minnie was a blend of beauty from her mother's roots and her father's European background. She spoke fluent Spanish and Zapotec.

In Juchitán, women ran both business and government, while men looked after the home and children. This formula worked. I use past tense because I'm not sure how much of it has been eroded over the years.

The commonalities among matriarchal societies worldwide are many, but most importantly, rape or abuse of women are non-existent, wars are unheard of, and disputes are easily resolved in the best interest of everyone involved.

If only we promoted the advancement of women and feminine goddess energy in leadership, what a different world we'd live in.

My love of solitude, and mistrust of others led me to have one or two friends at most – one at school and one at home. I didn't need any more. Plus the thought of maintaining more friendships gave me anxiety. Even today, my circle of friends is small, but tight.

I was protective of myself and my personal space and had a hard time letting strangers in.

I was also afraid of being seen, and it wasn't till I was in my forties that I realized why I had tried so hard to be invisible my entire life.

Invisibility had affected the corporate opportunities I went after, relationships, friendships, life choices and business decisions.

I always assumed it had to do with being shy, but realized it had more to do with self-preservation.

My unconscious mind had been programmed by childhood trauma.

I tell clients that people behave in the ways that they didn't deal with their childhood trauma.

To be seen as a child meant to be beaten by my maternal grandfather. So, I hid from everyone in relationships and jobs, and avoided being put in the spotlight at all costs.

My only 'sanctuary' was Grandma Minnie.

Shortly after I turned a year old, my mom dropped my sister, brother and I off at Grandma Minnie's home.

She said she had to finish her law degree. She was only 22 with three kids under the age of four; two of whom were hearing impaired.

She came back for us when I turned four and took us to live with her parents, while she saved up enough money to buy a place of her own.

I'm not sure why my mother came back for us. The rumor going around in the toxic family grapevine was that she felt guilty after being hit head on by a drunk driver and left for dead on the side of the highway after a night out with friends. But, I know she loved us in her own way.

"Always slow down at intersections, especially at night, even if you have a green light," she warned me when I started driving at seventeen.

Lucky for me, I followed her advice and it saved my life on a few occasions.

My mother's parents' home was right out of a horror movie.

On one side, there was my grandfather Victor, an angry neurotic man who despised my father and projected his unresolved anger towards us.

"Your father is an abuser!" He'd yell as he chased us around the house to beat us any time my siblings did something that displeased him, which was daily.

I don't think he ever considered himself an abuser.

Ironic, I know.

I think our mere existence annoyed him, especially my brother's.

Andrew was the mirror image of my father, even though my father often claimed that we were not his.

Another irony.

I laughed each time he insinuated that. I think it was his own way of justifying the fact that he had been a terrible father to us.

My sister, Monica was a year older; my brother, Andrew, two years my senior.

They were hearing impaired, but my brother was also autistic, although autism wasn't diagnosed until much later in life. His schizophrenia was diagnosed after he suffered a nervous breakdown at the age of sixteen.

Although I was the youngest of what I refer to as the first 'brood' in my father's offspring, I was treated as the 'oldest' for several reasons.

I was given the responsibility of looking after my siblings, and I took it full on. I was their protector, translator, warning bell, guide, and surrogate parent.

There was an Arctic-like atmosphere at my maternal grandparents' house. The floors were made of cold white marble, which they covered up with hunter green carpet so we wouldn't ruin their precious and expensive floors.

The furniture was covered in plastic from top to bottom to keep us from ruining it.

Crocheted tablecloths with a glass tabletop adorned the tables in the living room, dining room and kitchen.

Some people baby-proof their homes. They people-proofed theirs.

The temperature in the house was always cool, as if to keep everyone from getting too comfortable and always on our toes.

The only noises that could be heard were those of my grandfather's belt striking our skin or my brother's head, his insults, or when we were lucky, the sound of the TV.

No music was ever heard in that house.

The blackout curtains kept the sunshine out. The patio was desolate.

The food we were fed was often past due or rotting, and it wasn't until I could prove that it was indeed decayed, that they would stop trying to force us to eat it.

The concept of, "If it's yellow, let it mellow. If it's brown, flush it down," applied when it came to water conservation in the washrooms.

We also had to be conscious of collecting gray water in the shower and use it to flush the toilets.

Lights had to be turned off, unless absolutely necessary.

Today, I'm grateful for the environmental conservation education because it made me environmentally conscious, but I didn't particularly enjoy the way in which the lesson was delivered.

My siblings and I couldn't wait for the weekend to arrive, so we could escape their martial laws and take refuge in Grandma Minnie's sanctuary.

I played with my dolls in my room, purposely staying out of sight, laying low or hiding in a closet, so I wouldn't be included in the one-for-all, all-for-one beatings that were Grandfather Victor's favorite pastime.

He and his wife, Angela, were retired school teachers.

I felt sorry for anyone who had been their student before they retired, and wondered how they'd treated them.

I guess he figured his heavy hand would set an example and make us think twice before setting him off, but it didn't work. Monica and Andrew always pissed him off.

I was jealous when I saw how he treated my mom's sisters' kids. Grandfather Victor was a completely different man with them.

At night, I shared a dark, somber room with my siblings, which would fill with spirits that preyed on me.

One of the spirits stood at the foot of my bed. The other, a woman resembling 'Maleficent,' would appear in the midst of darkness and stare at me from the side of my bed.

I felt them before I saw them.

Every cell in my body shivered. I pulled the sheets over my head, hoping and praying for them to go away, but they wouldn't.

The spirit at the end of my bed held my feet down, while Maleficent pressed down on my chest or held my shoulders down.

At first, I hoped they were nightmares, but realized that for nightmares to occur, one has to be asleep. These things happened when I was fully awake.

Terrified to go to sleep at night, I often waited for my mother to get back from work late in the evening, so she could rub my back until I fell asleep on her bed. Then, she'd carry me to my bed.

But the ghosts were always there when I woke up in the middle of the night, and they often woke me up by grabbing parts of my body.

We lived in that house till I turned eight, when my mom bought a three-bedroom condo and we were finally able to escape from what I considered hell.

Our new home was much more conducive to relaxation and a sense of 'safety' for me. I didn't sense any negative spirits there, so I could focus on being a kid and playing with the new friends we made in the neighborhood.

My mom still forced us to visit her parents sometimes, but we usually opted to go to Grandma Minnie's home on weekends, as well as summer and winter vacations.

Being an empath, I've always found it difficult to go into crowds or malls. That is, until I figured out how to protect my energy by bringing my aura in and using an energy bubble.

I realized that the reason I often repelled people, or caused jealousy or envy, was because when we resonate at a high vibration, we repel those who vibrate at lower vibrations or are in a negative state.

This isn't to say that haven't negative myself at times. But for the most part, I am conscious of it and do my best to get back to a positive resonance, even during the darkest moments of my life when I couldn't see the light at the end of the tunnel.

More and more, I began to notice that certain environments, people and music were more conducive to my inner peace, especially places like lakes, rivers or generally in nature.

Once I had that figured out, I made a consistent effort to only surround myself with people, sounds, things and environments that contribute to high vibrations.

I have to admit that I've come across people in my life who felt they couldn't be my friend because of my gifts. The idea terrified them.

Even some of my family members have stopped communication with me because I chose to be open about my gifts.

I don't feel bad about any of it. Their choices cannot influence my self-worth or deter me from my path. Thankfully, I don't live for the validation of others.

The work that I do requires courage in many ways.

...

As I mentioned earlier, my hope is for you to reflect on your own miraculous experiences.

Before I take you to the first miraculous moment that defined my life in the next chapter, I'd like you to take some time to reflect.

Reflection Time:

Let me start by asking, how different did you feel as a child?

Do you understand that you were different for a reason and that it is what makes you so unique today?

Take the time to write down on a piece of paper the qualities that make you special. It's an awesome exercise to acknowledge them and honor them.

If you ever feel out of sorts, read this list. It's your resource list, a reminder of how capable and unique you are.

The First Miracle

I always had differing views about religion from those of my Grandmother Minnie, a devout Catholic.

She went to church every Sunday, attending daily in her later years.

She wanted me to attend church with her, but I refused. Well, at least when I had a choice in the matter.

At the age of three, I didn't really have a choice, but as soon as I was able to prevent people from physically dragging me to church, I stopped going.

My siblings and I spent a lot of time with Grandma Minnie by choice, but also because she became our primary caretaker when my mom abandoned us the first time.

Grandma Minnie was a tenacious woman, fantastic at business, self-confident and resilient, so whenever she had the opportunity, she asked me to at least pray with her in front of the figure of the Sacred Heart that hung on the dining room wall.

To her disappointment, I'd turn the invitation down, "God is inside of me Grandma, and God and I have a special relationship. I don't have to go to church or pray."

I did, however, bring miniature roses from my paternal grandfather's rose garden once a week in the early morning hours and placed them in the Sacred Heart's hands. I did it because the flowers looked and smelled lovely, not in reverence to God. Regardless, it made Grandma Minnie happy.

In an attempt to sway my opinion, she'd remind me that I should be grateful because it was thanks to God and the Sacred Heart that the middle finger of my right hand was healed. The details of which are ahead in this chapter.

Some may argue that it was my grandmother's healing energy that healed my finger, but it makes no difference, really. We are all part of God anyway.

When I was old enough to argue back, I'd hold my middle finger up, responding with a pinch of attitude, "It's not intact. God didn't do that great of a job. He left it crooked."

Even when I took it upon myself to read the Bible and she got excited, I brought her expectations down by saying, "Grandma, I'm only reading it to know what it says as a great piece of literature, but not for the reasons you're hoping."

The religious battle between us continued until my grandma's death in 2005. She tried to reinforce something in me that was already there, just not the way she expected me to reflect it.

The story of my first miracle became a family legend.

It was shortly after I turned three in 1971. Grandma Minnie and I, along with two of my uncles, Jose and Juan, who were in their twenties, were getting into Uncle Juan's Pacer to go shopping downtown.

I never liked that car because it looked weird. Rounded bubbled windows didn't seem to fit with the look of a regular car, but it was all the rage, so my grandmother bought it for Uncle Juan.

Grandma Minnie didn't drive, so the men in the family took turns driving her places, or she took taxis or public transportation.

The Rolling Stones' Jumpin' Jack Flash was playing on the radio.

The sky was clear and the sun was bright.

Mexico City's weather is warmest and driest in March and April, when the heat is almost unbearable. However, the months of July and August are usually rainy and cool. Even if it's sunny during the day, you're guaranteed monsoon rain in the evening and overnight.

I was wearing a fancy coat and patent leather shoes.

Grandma Minnie looked flawless in a two-piece camel color suit, a matching purse and 1.5" square toe high heels.

My uncles proudly wore flared jeans, corduroy jackets, platform shoes and large sunglasses.

They almost looked like twins, except one was the shade of coffee and the other, milk.

Uncle Jose had light skin like Grandma Minnie. Uncle Juan had dark skin, like Grandma Minnie's mother, my great-grandmother Maria, definitely not like my paternal grandfather. My paternal grandfather, Armando, was so fair, he was almost transparent.

I admired my uncles' and grandma's sense of style even at that age.

Uncle Jose got into the driver's seat. I was the second-last to get into the backseat on the passenger side with the help of Uncle Juan.

I sat down. Uncle Juan pushed his seat back and got into the car.

He closed the door, unaware that my right hand was still holding on to the car's door frame.

In a fraction of a second, the world seemed to close in on me.

I screeched, turning my head to look at my grandmother with helpless desperation as pain and shock began to take over my tiny body.

My face was the color of dark crimson. I felt like I couldn't breathe.

"Open the door!" Grandma Minnie yelled.

Uncle Juan, unaware of what had just occurred, immediately opened the door and got out of the car to investigate.

"You crushed her hand!" yelled my grandmother.

He leaned towards me for a closer inspection. His hands began to tremble.

The middle finger of my tiny little hand was mangled.

I pulled my hand towards me. I saw blood, flesh and bone, but had no idea what that meant, only how it felt.

Tears flowed down my face like a turbulent river of unbearable pain.

Uncle Juan turned into a statue, frozen by guilt and disbelief.

A fraction of a second later, my grandmother pulled me into her arms.

She held my hand in her hand as tight as possible to try to stop the bleeding, and to prevent me from seeing the damage.

Then she carried me back inside the house as she yelled, "Go get Dr. Martinez!"

My uncles wasted no time. They ran to Doctor Martinez's home just a few streets away.

In the meantime, Grandma Minnie walked as fast as she could towards the dining room, stopping in front of the Sacred Heart that hung on the wall.

She held me in a warm embrace as she prayed, swaying from side to side, holding my right hand tightly in hers.

She prayed and repeated over and over that everything would be OK.

After what seemed like a lifetime, my uncles arrived with the doctor.

There was a trail of blood on the floor from the car to the house.

My wailing had decreased to whimpers.

Uncle Juan's hands were still shaking.

As they got closer to us, Grandma Minnie continued to pray, swaying side to side in a trance.

Dr. Martinez had to place his hand on her shoulder to get her attention.

She stopped and turned towards him.

"May I see her hand, please?"

My grandmother gently loosened her grip on my right hand.

He looked at both our hands and then looked up at my grandmother. Both our hands were covered in blood.

He proceeded to place his index finger on my hand to feel the blood. It was warm.

I pulled my hand away.

He grabbed my hand again gently. I pulled away. He grabbed it again. I stopped resisting and rested my head against my grandmother's chest as I whimpered.

Dr. Martinez turned my hand in several directions to examine it.

He looked at me and my grandmother again with bewilderment and proceeded to grab a handkerchief from his pocket to wipe the blood off his fingers.

Then, as if running out of options about what to think, he turned to my uncles, who were standing slightly to his side, looking over his shoulder.

My grandmother smiled at them, brought my tiny hand to her lips and kissed it.

My uncles dropped their jaws in amazement.

My grandmother took my hand very slowly and extended it towards them.

I pulled my hand back and hugged my grandmother tightly.

"I thought you said she had mangled her finger?" Dr. Martinez turned towards my uncles.

"She did!" Uncle Juan, still full of guilt and fear, was quick to respond, without a clue as to how to explain what they were witnessing.

Uncle Jose placed both hands on his head in complete disbelief.

"But she's perfectly fine, aside from the blood," Dr. Martinez assured them.

"It's a miracle," my grandmother interjected with absolute confidence.

"What do you mean?" Dr. Martinez asked.

"I prayed to the Sacred Heart," she said.

The doctor raised his eyebrows and scratched his head, "I don't think there's anything I can do. Her hand and fingers seem to be intact."

My uncles walked him towards the front door and thanked him for coming over.

He left, not quite sure what to think of the ordeal, but my grandmother didn't need validation from anyone.

My finger had healed instantaneously, although a bit crooked, with a mild curvature on the middle finger as a lifelong reminder of the power of Source energy (love), intention and *belief*.

My grandmother's healing intention and her blind trust in God's power were unstoppable.

The only scar I was left with was my hesitation towards car doors and Pacer cars, the latter of which was thankfully discontinued not long afterwards.

However, my stance on going to church didn't change much over the years, right up until my grandmother's passing.

...

But God wasn't about to let me forget about the special relationship we had.

Years later, I would be reminded of the true meaning of, and the strength of my connection to God in The Miracle of The Sacred Heart in the chapter ahead.

Reflection Time:

What would it take for you to believe in God's power, or your own power?

Dig deep into the archives of your long-term memory. Are there any instances where you could attribute an outcome to an unseen force?

If you can't believe, what is blocking you? Is it resistance to the idea of God or Source that is within you?

The Miracle of The Sacred Heart

Fast-forward 44 years to 2015.

Even though I refused to go into churches as a child, I've always found them peaceful places for meditation. They also provided a quiet escape from the hectic pace of everyday life in Mexico City.

The irony of this is that although I joked with my grandmother that if I ever went into a church, it would likely go up in flames, the complete opposite occurs when I do.

My energetic field becomes much stronger in churches. I start to glow and feel my aura spread far and wide around me, as well as beams of light that shoot out of my hand and crown chakras.

On a sunny autumn day, I found myself walking around downtown Mexico City, enjoying the subtle warmth of the sun on my skin when I came across a particular chapel I discovered in Mexico City years ago, where I could take refuge and meditate.

The chapel was unique in the sense that it didn't stand out. Half of it had been destroyed by an earthquake, so only part of the structure remained.

As I got closer to it, I noticed a car with bubble windows parked on the street. It was a Pacer.

I cringed. The memory of my finger being caught in the door flashed in my head. I felt a knot in my stomach.

I immediately thought of the effect that traumatic memories can have on the body, so I took a deep breath to release that somatic response as I continued walking towards the chapel.

I didn't even know if it would be open, but when I arrived, it was.

The inside was small and unpretentious, with only a few pews.

The only sounds that could be heard were the echoing of my feet on the ground.

There was only one other person in there, a man sitting close to the entrance.

The chapel lacked a typical identifier in Mexican church walls: images of a crucified bloody Jesus surrounded by the opulence of gold.

There was only a tall statue of the Son of God behind the altar, but no blood anywhere.

Part of the reason I was there was to ask for help from God because I felt as if I'd been placed in a concrete room without a window. My life seemed to have reached a phase of stagnation and flat-out defeat that I couldn't seem to unblock with my bad-ass manifesting abilities.

I'd also recently been told by a local doctor that after months of trying to stop my uterus from hemorrhaging, there was nothing more that could be done.

The problem had advanced so much that I was losing about 2L of blood every month. I learned that the human body only replenishes about a liter of blood per month.

"I have no idea why you're still alive. However, what I do know is that you're about to go into total organ failure. I don't know if you have hours, days or maybe weeks, but you're most certainly going to die. I cannot even do an emergency hysterectomy because you wouldn't survive the operation. You have no hemoglobin or iron left in your body. The only thing I may be able to do is a full blood transfusion, but you'll have to get the donors yourself. There are no blood banks in Mexico."

The words I heard from his mouth seemed foreign to me. He may as well have been speaking another language.

I wasn't afraid of dying. However, the option of finding donors was out of the question. My dad was a priority and he was in and out of emergency at least once every other month from the effects of kidney failure.

I'd gone through my medical challenges in silence and alone. I didn't want my family to worry any more than they already did with my dad being sick.

I had to get back to Canada as soon as possible because that was my home now, and if I was going to die, I wanted to die there.

I looked around the chapel, paying close attention to as many details as I could because I had no idea if I'd ever get a chance to visit again in physical form.

I focused on the wood of the heavy entrance doors, and looked closely at the stained windows with pictorial representations of the life of Christ, the supporting images of saints on the walls, and the focal point at center stage, a massive figure of Jesus.

I took my time choosing a place to sit. There was no need to rush.

I sat down half way up the pews, close to the outer edge.

I took a deep breath and closed my eyes as I organized my thoughts in preparation for my conversation with God.

I got down on my knees and placed my hands on the edge of the pew in front of me with my palms facing upwards.

This is part of my ritual for establishing my connection with the Divine. Getting on my knees is my way of surrendering. Placing my hands this way is like an 'on' switch that helps me become aware of my connection to Source.

Immediately, I felt and saw the energy shooting upwards from my hands and felt the energy from my Crown chakra shooting upwards into the Universe.

Whenever I do this, the energy is so strong that I feel like I'm being lifted upwards like a marionette.

"God, I've done everything I could to find the right partner, have a successful business, be healthy, get to know my father on a deeper level and have a functional relationship with him and my family, but nothing seems to be going right. I feel lost. I don't know what else to do, so I *surrender* . I leave this in your capable hands and trust that you're way more skilled at finding solutions to all of these issues than I am. Please help me. If I am meant to die, give me enough time to get home, but if I am meant to live, guide me to the people who will help me heal."

At that moment, I felt the energy from my hands and Crown chakra become stronger, expanding outwards all around me.

Suddenly, I felt a blanket of unconditional loving energy surround me, embracing me into a cocoon of safety.

It was the most intense, beautiful energy I've ever felt in my life, so intense that I couldn't help but release a gentle stream of reciprocal loving tears.

My body felt light, freed from the emotional weight that had anchored it in darkness for so long.

At that moment, I realized that this was the 'bliss' that monks talked about while atop the Himalayan mountains after years of intense meditation practice.

I was in awe that someone like me, a mere mortal who'd been such a rebel, could experience such a beautiful and spiritual connection to Source energy.

Immediately, I became aware that no one – not my father, mother, grandmother, a lover or partner, friends, unborn children, siblings or pets, could give me this type or intensity of love. The only thing I ever needed to do in order to feel the intensity of Source Love, was to maintain my awareness of my connection to God.

We're never disconnected from Source. It is our awareness of the connection that is lost.

This knowing was so simple and yet, so elusive.

I understood at that moment that I had the power to feel this tremendously powerful connection to Source energy any time, any place, under any circumstance, as long I got out of my own way.

Then came the realization that I had to stop sacrificing myself for others without regard for myself.

The Universe loves balance and I could no longer continue giving without receiving.

I had to turn the caring, compassion, kindness and love inward. I had to learn to love myself **unconditionally**.

I finally realized that I had to open myself up to receive love, abundance and intimacy, as well as healthy friendships and relationships.

The gentle tears became entangled with a smile that gladly led the exodus of emotions towards the *Light* .

I had my answers.

"If I die now, I'll die the happiest person on the planet. I don't know what I did to deserve this, but thank you. *Thank you* !"

I wiped my tears and looked around. I was one of three people in the chapel now.

Phew! No one in the chapel had become aware of what had just transpired - another miraculous moment with God.

My body still felt light. I let out a sigh of relief, feeling renewed. I gathered myself together, and as if picking myself off the ground, got up slowly and walked towards the front doors.

Gratitude oozed out of my pores.

When I reached the entrance, I decided to look around again to see if I could find the name of this very special chapel.

I wonder why I like this church so much?

I had tried to find its name during previous visits without any luck.

Then, as I turned my head to the right, I noticed a brass plaque on the wall, which I was certain had been there all along, but for some reason, I had not noticed it prior to this moment.

It read, *"***Chapel of The Sacred Heart.***"*

I paused and read it again, and again and again. I stood there looking at it like a deer staring at a set of headlights on the road.

Then I made my way back inside the chapel, taking my time examining each of the images of Jesus on the walls, until I was back at the entrance. They were all different images of The Sacred Heart, which are images of Jesus with his heart on his chest vs. inside.

This image symbolizes many things in the Catholic religion, including Jesus' sacrifice for humanity, the love that Jesus has for his

Father and humanity, but more importantly, the essence of God's energy, which is *Divine and unconditional love* .

I turned my head slowly to find the tall statue of Jesus behind the altar.

It was a statue of The Sacred Heart.

How did I not notice this before?

Suddenly, it dawned on me why there were no signs of blood or pain or suffering anywhere in the chapel. This chapel was a sanctuary representing God's love.

This was no coincidence and I knew it.

I stood in front of the brass plaque by the entrance and read again, **"Chapel of The Sacred Heart."**

I took a deep slow breath, raised my right hand, looked at my crooked middle finger and smiled.

Just like that, gentle tears made their way down my face again.

I looked up at the plaque and thought, *"Grandma, YOU ARE GOOD! I mean, really good!"*

Shortly after that, I went home to Canada to focus on healing.

When I told a friend who never misses a Sunday at church this story, and her response was, "I know that you believe what you're saying, but I find it really hard to believe that any of this is possible."

I didn't try to convince her that the experience actually happened. I just smiled and changed the subject.

I find it futile to try to convince anyone of anything.

It's not up to us to make believers out of non-believers, even if they go to church every Sunday and preach the Gospel, yet fail to believe the concept that we are all part of the same Source energy, and that miracles are real, and that they happen to all people, not just Jesus.

…

This story doesn't end here. The Miracle of Self-Love in Chapter 28 goes deeper into my miraculous recovery, but before we get there, I'll introduce you to my first official mentor in the following chapter - the woman who would awaken my curiosity in the field of quantum physics.

Reflection Time:

Take a moment to look back at your life experiences.

Are there moments which you dismissed as 'coincidence' that could be considered miracles, big or small?

How has this story helped you to look at situations differently?

My First Sensei

Toni was my mom's aunt on her father's side of the family. She was my grandfather's cousin and was raised in the USA.

She was married to an American-born lawyer, who worked for one of the big three car manufacturers at the time in Detroit, MI.

She refused to let anyone call her "aunt" or "mom". She was just, 'Toni.'

She and her husband, Stewart, lived in a large ranch-style bungalow in a quiet and quaint suburb of Detroit, now called Beverly Hills.

I got to visit them on weekends while I attended the University of Windsor, across the Detroit River.

They were separated, but lived in the same house. She lived upstairs and he took up residence in the basement. The arrangement worked for them.

Having been through my parents' toxic relationship and subsequent poisonous divorce, I couldn't believe that people like Toni and Stewart existed, or that they could be happy and respectful to each other living in the same home.

She and her husband remained friends, even though they were separated, and both were OK with the other dating other people.

When they went to events with their son, they each brought their respective partners, and their son introduced them as, "This is Toni and her lover," and "This is my dad and his lover."

My mom introduced me to Toni in hopes that she'd keep an 'eye' on me while I was at school.

It was 1987. I was 19 years old, and although I'd been admitted to two other universities closer to home, I picked the one furthest away.

Toni suffered from alopecia, so she wore wigs.

The first time she took her wig off in front of me, it took me by surprise, but I quickly got used to it.

She told me a funny story about how she was on her way to a dinner with very important people one evening, but was running late and forgot to secure her wig with glue.

So, when she got out of her car at the event, her wig went flying and she had to chase after it.

She put it back on and walked into the event, calm and collected.

Toni was an accomplished woman with a Ph.D. in physics and a specialization in artificial intelligence. She was also a gifted psychic, who worked for the US Military on top secret projects because of her scientific credentials, but also because of her psychic abilities.

Although she said she couldn't give me many details about her top-secret job, she told me way more than I ever expected.

She worked on projects which required the highest levels of security clearance, including controlled remote viewing (CRV).

Controlled remote viewing is a systematized protocol that allows the psychic viewer to 'see' places, events and people in the past, present or future.

This method is used by governments around the world to spy on each other.

Technically, it's an extra-sensory technique, but because it's used by the military, it was developed as a strict protocol for comparative analysis.

The viewer is given number coordinates representing the target, and uses a type of shorthand to tune into the target, and by feeling the shorthand symbols, the reader is able to sense different aspects of the target and describe it. Hence the name, "controlled remote viewing."

Toni's living room in her ranch-style bungalow became a 'classroom' of sorts during my visits.

She'd make tea and shared her knowledge with me.

She mesmerized me by sharing her knowledge about quantum physics, time travel and secret societies.

She talked about how the 'one percent' (the elite who truly rule the world) have infiltrated every major organization around the globe, including Olympic Committees, governments, top corporations, and Hollywood.

She spoke of psychic abilities, parallel universes, the fact that time doesn't exist (past, present and future exist at the same time), the paranormal, the spirit world and her energy healing abilities.

She explained, "We are nothing but space. Every atom is separated by space. Our minds fill in the space and condense the atoms so that our logical mind can make sense of the information, but if you could see yourself with a different set of glasses, you'd see that we're nothing but a great big holograph. If you were to compress the atoms of every single person on earth, they'd fit nicely into a cube of sugar."

What?

Toni gave me more details about remote viewing and the concept of parallel universes, as well as how she was able to tap into the 'field' to determine outcomes.

"What I am able to 'see' as a psychic is based on parallels," she continued. "Every decision we make can keep us on the same parallel or switch us to another, thus change the outcome. So in essence, what I am able to 'see' when I read someone, something or a situation, is based on the decisions that led to that parallel, but at any time, they can change the outcome by making another decision and hence, switch to another parallel."

It was all so fascinating!

She went deeper, "I'm often asked to determine the outcome of a military tactic for strategic planning purposes in military operations. They use me to plan wars and determine the outcome of specific strategies."

I could not get enough.

She continued, "Nothing is cast in stone. All the possible outcomes exist at the same time, as does past, present, and future. There's no separation of time or space in the quantum field. So, when you're here, you're there and everywhere at the same time. Governments all over the world, and the people who rule the world, know this and utilize psychics to plan their wars. However, all of it is hush-hush. Not many people even know we exist within the military."

When I watched Dr. Steven Greer's documentaries, 'Unacknowledged' and 'Close Encounters of the Fifth Kind', I was relieved that the information Toni had shared with me was finally public.

One of the biggest lessons she taught me was, "If anyone ever does any wrong unto you, never, ever wish them ill because if you do, you'll be wishing it unto yourself, and it will come back to you with twice the force. It's called the boomerang effect. Instead, wish them what they deserve and the Universe will take care of the rest. Source knows what each of us deserves."

The Boomerang Effect is based on the concept that for every action, there's an equal and opposite reaction (Newton's Law).

Toni taught me how to protect my energy by visualizing an energy shield with a reflective mirror surface on the outside.

She said, "Set the intention that anything that doesn't serve you be reflected back to its source."

I've used it ever since.

She went on to detail how she'd treated herself with energy medicine after being diagnosed with a large tumor in one of her breasts.

Doctors in the US had recommended a double mastectomy.

She refused and instead visualized the tumor being encapsulated to prevent it from metastasizing.

A few weeks later, she travelled to Mexico and instructed local surgeons at a private hospital to remove only the tumor.

Once she recovered from the anesthetic, the doctors showed her the tumor, which she'd asked them to preserve for her.

They'd sent the tissue to pathology and were surprised at the findings, "Your tumor is encased in a material that we have yet to identify. It is not on any databases ever recorded in medicine. However, it seems to have stopped the tumor from metastasizing."

My eyes widened.

"I set the intention for the tumor to be contained and my body knew exactly what to do," Aunt Toni said with confidence.

"There was no need for chemo or radiation either. The human body is remarkable."

Toni taught me about brain wave frequencies and how to go into Alpha and Theta with a simple technique.

Then she showed me how to use energy medicine to heal myself and others, as well as use spirit guides and tune into the soul of living guides to do so.

More than thirty years later, when I came across The Silva Method, by John Silva, I realized Toni had taught me everything she knew from the Silva Method about manifestation and self-healing.

Those teachings would come in very handy in the year 2000, nine years before I certified in Reiki level 1 and 2.

"If you ever want to know something, all you have to do is put on the corresponding 'hat' for that knowledge."

I turned my head sideways like a puppy.

"For example, if you ever want to know how to use a photography camera, just put on your imaginary photographer's hat and you'll get access to that knowledge."

"That's it?"

"Yes."

"How do I know I'm not making it up?"

"Because we all have access to that knowledge. It's in the Field and all you have to do to remember it, is access it. The 'hats' are just a way to set that intention for the information to be downloaded to you."

I was mesmerized.

This, by the way, is also known as quantum jumping.

"Now, I'm going to show you how to perform psychic surgery."

"What?" I said.

"You're going to put on your surgeon's hat."

"OK," I said with hesitation and anticipation at the same time.

"Close your eyes. Go into Theta frequency."

I did.

"Now visualize yourself taking an elevator to the basement of a building. You're entering a room and in the middle of that room is a surgical table."

"OK."

"Who are you going to perform surgery on, yourself or someone else?"

"Can I perform surgery on myself?"

"Of course! In the quantum field, everything is possible."

"OK, then me."

"Alright. Lay your body on the table. Now put your surgeon's hat on your energetic body, which is standing beside the table."

"OK."

"What would you like to work on?"

"My right knee."

"What's wrong with your right knee?"

"I injured it in my first day of dance class at school and the physiotherapist at the university said I'll never be able to dance again."

"OK, set the intention to heal your right knee. It's time to call your guides in. Who would you like to call in?"

"I don't know. Can it be anyone, alive or dead?"

"Yes. In the quantum field, there is no difference between dead or alive, incarnated or spirit, past vs. present vs. future. Remember, it's all energy and it's all happening at the same time. The concepts of time or separation are only concepts. They don't actually exist in the quantum field."

"I suppose my great aunt Lana, who passed away, then my dad and my grandma."

"Anyone else?"

"Can it be strangers too?"

"Yes."

"Cool! OK that's it for now."

"OK. Ask your dad and grandmother to assist you. The moment you do this, their energy will appear in the room."

"They're beside me."

"Great. They already know what to do, as do you. Remember, you put on your surgeon's hat."

I proceeded to perform psychic surgery on my right knee, not really knowing if I was doing the right things or not, but somehow trusting that I was.

I visualized a scalpel and proceeded to open the skin over my knee, slowly and with extreme care. I felt like a surgeon. All of this was happening in my head, of course.

I went in and scraped away lose material that was causing my patella from gliding properly.

My grandmother, great aunt Lana and my dad observed and handed me the tools I needed, but I realized they were there more for moral support. I already 'knew' what I had to do.

I closed my energetic knee with imaginary stitches, and my knee healed instantaneously from the sutures.

No scar was left.

My knee felt amazing as I took the imaginary elevator up with my guides.

"What if everything is wrong with me? What if I wanted to give myself a completely new body?" I asked.

"Then give yourself a new body. There are no limits in the quantum field."

I have to clarify that my knee pain recurred intermittently over the years until I did acupuncture a few years later.

I've learned a few things since, and one of them is that we need to be consistent with energy treatments, especially with more serious injuries or conditions.

The other is that sometimes the body heals faster with a wholistic approach that treats the physical, mental, emotional and energetic bodies.

I never asked Toni why she hadn't healed her alopecia with energy. It just wasn't a priority for me, but as I think back, I assume that she either hadn't put much effort into it, or other priorities took precedence in her life. I doubt it was because she didn't care about her looks because she did.

Toni exuded confidence unlike any other person I'd ever met.

"You know, most of the women in our family are fearless."

My grandfather's sisters and cousins were independent, competitive and athletic, but I appreciated Toni's tenacity and class, and secretly thanked my mother for introducing me to whom I considered to be the coolest, most intelligent and fascinating woman on the planet.

Toni also took it upon herself to groom me into a 'lady.'

On one of the weekends that Toni invited me to spend time with her, she picked me up from my dorm on a snowy Saturday, dressed in a track suit and high heel black boots, which was unusual for her because she was always well-dressed.

"We're going to Saks 5th Avenue."

"OK" I said, not caring a bit about our destination. I just wanted to spend time with her.

"Today's lesson is to show you just how different people will treat you dressed a certain way."

"Does it really matter?"

"Absolutely, which is the reason for today's lesson."

I guess she too, agreed with Grandma Minnie's complaints that ripped jeans and a t-shirt weren't acceptable in our family, especially being a Mexican woman.

She'd often look at me as I was about to leave with her and say, "No self-respecting woman would ever walk out the door looking like that," or "Are you going like that? Oh, no. Go change. Now."

I knew exactly what I needed to look like if I wanted to be seen in public with my grandmother.

When we got to Saks, Toni got out of the car, opened the passenger door on her side and pulled out a beautiful, long black fur coat.

She wore it over her pink velour track suit. Her black boots covered up the track suit from the floor up.

She was glamorous even when she dressed 'down.'

We walked together into the store. She took slow, calculated strides as she walked, each with precise timing, commanding her presence.

We made our way down the main corridor between cosmetics and perfumes.

"Watch and learn," she said as she increased her speed and walked just a bit ahead of me with her head held high.

I slowed down so I could watch as instructed.

Right away, every sales person who noticed her stopped what they were doing and headed towards her with offers of one perfume sample, then another, which she kindly took from them and smiled graciously.

I was invisible to them when I walked past them.

She turned to look at me and smiled.

When I caught up to her, she said, "You see?"

I smiled, "Yes."

"None of them have any idea of what I'm wearing underneath. They simply see what I have on top and it screams, 'MONEY' and 'POWER.' You need to choose how you want to be treated by society. The way you express yourself, your accent, your vocabulary, enunciation, pronunciation, the way you walk, the way you move, drive, behave, your clothes – all of it will determine how people treat you. Always command respect."

"OK." It was a lot to process, especially considering my rebellion against elitism.

The following week, she took me to a fancy restaurant a couple of hours from my school on the Canadian side, which she knew quite well because of all the travelling she did.

On the way, she taught me how to hold the wheel of a car like a 'lady.'

At the restaurant, she deepened my knowledge of table etiquette and more: all the things I'd rejected as part of my education in an all-girl British private school in Mexico.

I felt like Eliza Doolittle in "Pygmalion."

My English, however, was flawless. As a means of survival in a new culture, I'd worked hard to learn it and polish it to a point where I couldn't even fake a Mexican accent.

I envisioned her having dinner with the rich and famous, moving her hands with grace, observing everyone, reading each person, knowing exactly what to say to whom.

Shortly thereafter, Toni's only son, who was doing his dissertation in nuclear medicine at a world-renowned hospital, passed away suddenly from an apparent heart attack, while exercising on his stationary bike at home. He was only 33.

After his passing, I wasn't able to spend as much time with Toni.

Not only was she dealing with the grief of losing her only son, but her daughter-in-law was devastated, and Toni had to help her deal with the loss.

…

As I developed spiritually, I began to come across other teachers and guides, who eventually gave me answers with regards to past-life memories I'd had as a child or discovered during past-life regressions. I discuss this further in the next chapter.

Reflection Time:

Is there anyone in your life that influenced the way you see the world today in a significantly positive way? Maybe there are several people.

Have you taken an inventory of who they are and what you could thank them for, even if they're not around in physical form anymore?

Go ahead, make a list and take the time to acknowledge them and thank them energetically.

The Miracle of DNA Memories

I knew that our DNA and cells kept memories from our past lives before I read about it.

I just had this 'knowing' and trusted it, but only mentioned it to a chosen few because I knew they'd look at me like I had four heads, something which is quite common when you're intuitive.

'Knowing' is one of my gifts, otherwise referred to as claircognizance, the ability to have knowledge about situations or people without prior exposure to the information.

There could be no other explanation for the attraction I felt for certain places without ever having traveled to those places before.

Today, I understand that my attraction to Ireland, ballet, the French language, certain foods, French décor, music, piano, fencing, horses, dolphins, water, African drums and music, Turkey, Bali, Australia and other locations around the world, are because of my past life DNA memories.

Our DNA is like a computer motherboard and even if the data gets erased, it can always be recovered. It is also programmable and we have the power to program it with new instructions.

When it came to locations that called me, I felt like I knew them, or had been there when I saw pictures of them. Some of the places felt like 'home' and others felt familiar. The local foods tasted comforting. The sounds when I was there were soothing and the sensations in my body felt right when I looked at the surroundings, even when I looked at a photograph of them.

All of it was unexplainable, and a part of me knew that I carried those memories in my cells, which caused an attraction to them, like two magnets being pulled towards each other.

The magnetic pull makes total sense to me because at the core, we're also electrical beings made up of many minerals and fluids (water).

Everything that occurs in our body, every movement, our speech, hearing, all of it, is driven by the chemical reactions of those minerals and water (fluids), that create electrical charges.

This is also why it is so important for us to be fully hydrated. We are water and minerals for the most part, and in order for electrical impulses to travel, they need a conduction agent such as water.

Water keeps memories and carries information.

All the 'knowing' I've experienced in my life is just remembering what I already knew in those past lives and brought with me to this lifetime.

My Awareness of Past Life Memories

My recollection of past lives began around the age of five, when I walked into the kitchen looking for Grandma Minnie, who was busy cooking one of her delicious dishes.

Grandma was happiest pouring love into her food.

I could see the steam rising from the pot on the stove, slowly dissipating into the air.

The aroma rising from the pot traveled through the entire house like a magical wave soothing the soul.

She was about to place a wooden spoon into the pot to sample her Divine creation, when I said, "Hey, Mrs.! When I die, I want my ashes spread over the sea of Ireland."

My grandmother stopped, placing the wooden spoon to the side.

I had a really bad habit of referring to her as, "Hey, Mrs.!" and puling on her skirt to get her attention.

She lowered the flame, turned to me and asked, "What did you just say?"

I repeated myself.

She paused again, "First of all, why are you talking about death when you're only five? Second, do you know what ashes are? Third, do you even know where Ireland is?"

"I don't know grandma. I just want you to promise me that. I want my ashes spread over the sea of Ireland when I die. Please make sure that happens," and I walked away.

She stood there, stunned and speechless.

About a year later, I began to add an "er" to the end of every word I spoke in Spanish and spoke with a French accent.

"Casa-er."

"Vamos-er."

"Mañana-er."

My Grandmother Minnie, who had the patience of a saint, couldn't help but ask, "What on earth are you saying?"

"I'm speaking-er French, don't you know-er?"

"Are you now?"

"Yes."

"Why?"

"Pff…because-er I'm French, don't you know-er?"

"No, you're Mexican and you speak Spanish."

"No, I'm French and speak French."

"Do you know where France is?"

"No."

At the time, I had no idea that my great-grandmother on my maternal grandmother's side was half French and half Irish.

The family legend was that my Great-Grandmother Veronica had been the fruit of an out of wedlock union between an Irish soldier and a French upper-class woman.

Unfortunately, during those times, young women who became pregnant out of wedlock were often sent off to convents run by the Catholic Church, or to the homes of faraway relatives until they gave birth.

The children born out of wedlock were given up for adoption or raised by other family members.

Such was the fate of Great-Grandmother Veronica, who was adopted by a well-established Mexican family that owned several apartment buildings in the city.

The legend was a well-kept and taboo secret in the family, not because she'd been adopted, but because she married her adoptive brother.

The story had all the ingredients for a juicy period telenovela.

I found out about the long-kept family secret after spending a weekend at great-aunt Consuelo's home in a resort city called Cocoyoc, about 90 minutes outside of Mexico City.

Aunt Consuelo was Grandfather Victor's sister.

I had several great-aunts on both sides of the family, but most of the great-aunts I visited were on my mother's side, and all were strong women.

Aunt Consuelo, also a retired teacher, drove a Mustang and proudly stated, "Our family loves speed."

I secretly wished that I'd grow up to be as cool as she was. I'm not sure that it happened, as I have more of a tendency to walk into walls and trip over myself, but I was certainly rebellious.

When I look back, if the Universe loves balance, I'm certainly balanced. I'm a rebel, who walks into corners, but somehow manages to come out of it with grace.

Aunt Consuelo's main residence in the southern part of Mexico City, was a large stone structure that resembled a castle, with a pool, tennis court, and a badminton court in the backyard.

"You know, everyone thinks I inherited the money to buy my homes, but that's not so," she said proudly.

"I worked hard for all of it."

Consuelo had taken the time to build the entire family tree and delighted in educating me on our family's history.

"We are descendants from the Duke and Duchess of so and so of Spain, Viceroy so and so, and … and on your father's side, the Marquis of so and so…Our family came here from Spain many years ago on a boat. One of the girls on that boat had been entrusted to a priest by our family, but was raped during the voyage by the priest. So, the family pretty much broke all ties with the Catholic Church after that."

The story was fascinating, though I couldn't care less about the royal lines on either side of my family's tree.

"You know what else got passed on in this family?"

"No."

"Anger. Well, more like rage. Everyone in this family has a really bad temper."

That was hard for me to believe because no one else I knew had my grandfather's rage, but I took her word for it.

"Don't judge your mother too much for abandoning you. She didn't know any better. After all, that's what she grew up with."

"I don't understand."

"Your mother left you when you were very young and again when you were twelve."

"Yes."

"Well, she was abandoned by her parents too, at the age of twelve. Except, she was left to care for her three younger siblings, the youngest of whom was six months old."

"She was?"

"Yes. Your grandparents were not great parents. They wanted to continue living a single life. They often left their kids with me for six months at a time, while taking a break at another home, only 10 minutes away. They never even called once to check on their kids. Your mom had to look after a ten-year-old, eight-year-old, and a six-month-old all on her own."

She noticed the look of shock on my face.

"No one ever told you this?"

"No, my mom never talks about her childhood, and denies her father ever hit her, even though I saw him do it. She also says nothing when I talk about how he hit us when we lived there, so it's no wonder she's never said a word."

"Well, they did. So, before you judge her, try to understand her and the examples of parenthood she grew up with."

I felt as if someone had twisted the cap off a soda bottle after it had been shaken to release the compressed gas a little at a time.

The slight and controlled release of emotions towards my mother turned into empathy, and eventually compassion.

I always complained that I had to cook for my older sister and brother on the weekends when my mom left us in Canada.

Then I watched Master Chef kid's edition and the kids on the show put me to shame.

Show-offs!

I couldn't imagine having to look after a six-month-old on my own for six months at the age of twelve.

When I did the past life regression with my tough-love spiritual mentor Jack, I began to understand a lot about my past lives, including the very intricate relationship with my mother.

...

The following six chapters depict some of my most memorable past life recollections. But before we go there, let's take some time to reflect.

Reflection Time:

Do you remember if you had any past-life memories as a child?

If so, did you recognize them as such?

If not, do you know what they were now?

Have you since had flashes of what could be past-life recollections?

How do you believe knowing about your past lives could help you in your current life?

Prima Ballerina

At the age of seven, I asked my mom if I could take ballet lessons.

My sister, Monica was going to Hawaiian dance lessons, so I figured I could go to ballet.

Not only that, but my mom was very supportive of sports activities, being athletic herself.

"No. I have no money. Ask your father to pay for them."

My excitement dwindled to the ground. However, I still had an alternative option: my father.

I waited with eager anticipation to see him on the weekend at Grandma Minnie's.

"No. I have no money. Tell your mother to pay for them."

My heart dropped.

Why didn't they ever have money? Were we poor? I didn't understand. They had good jobs and always had money for my sister's whims and my siblings' swimming lessons and trips, but never for anything that I asked for. Was I that much of a disappointment to them for not being a star athlete, that I didn't deserve to participate in activities that I liked?

It wasn't until years later that it dawned on me just how practical my mother was.

She enrolled all of us in the same extra-curricular activities, so she wouldn't be running all over the city as a taxi service.

Ah! *"All for one, and one for all."*

My father's reason for not paying for things was tied to his rationalization in his own mind that we weren't his and he wouldn't give into her manipulations.

Disappointed, but not defeated, I went into the TV den, which was a hub between four bedrooms and two washrooms at one end of my paternal grandparents' bungalow.

I closed the door behind me to keep potential interruptions at bay.

The space was mine, at least until after lunch, when the men in the family would come in to watch soccer.

I turned on the black and white television with only thirteen channels, and turned the knob to the channel that featured the Russian National Ballet every Sunday afternoon.

I loved music and dance more than anything. The moment I heard music play, I could feel it flow through my veins, and not in a figurative way. I felt it physically, its energy moving inside of me.

It made me feel so alive, vibrant and blissful!

No one was going to stop me from that.

What I didn't understand at such a young age, was that the yearning to learn ballet was really a pull towards a past life. I was remembering one of my passions in a past life and wanted to reconnect with it.

I watched, paying close attention to every sway, jump, step, leap, turn, and placement of their feet, legs, hips, hands, fingers, shoulders, chest and head.

I followed the pace of the dancers, not just with each other, but with themselves and a higher force; the same energy that made its way through my body and gave me goose bumps of joy.

I stood barefoot on my toes, holding my toothpick-thin arms parallel to the ground and then above my head like the ballerinas in front of me. I walked like them and moved like them.

I emulated them until I became them, losing myself in a world all my own.

In my head, I was not just a ballerina, I was a Prima Ballerina.

My aunts and uncles, unaware of my failed attempts at getting my parents to finance my dream, assumed I was going to ballet classes when they saw me 'practicing', never imagining that I was learning in alternative ways.

When I look back, I realize that I was just tuning into the skills I'd learned in a previous life.

I am grateful to my parents because their resistance to give in to my requests made me resourceful and resilient, almost to a fault.

Their responses to my requests and my subsequent actions that followed proved to me that no matter how many barriers we can encounter along the way, when something is meant to be and truly coming from inside of us, there will always be a way to reconnect with it.

A Connection to Horses

Whenever my mom took us camping throughout Mexico during the summer months, she rarely took us to an actual campsite.

She loved adventure and off-roading, so if she felt like settling in the middle of a farmer's field or a forest, beach, or any place with just enough flat ground to place a tent on, she would stop and set up camp.

Bathrooms were a luxury, so we had to develop an intimate relationship with holes in the ground, and the site had to be left as we found it.

Regardless of how rustic our accommodations were, the trips were always memorable.

I remember feeling a sense of being 'home', waking up just as the sun began to rise, and poking my head out of the tent to get a glimpse of the beauty of a field covered in a light mist and a thin layer of fog that gently hovered over the grass, following the contours of Mother Earth.

I'd take a deep breath, like a child coming out of a womb, grateful for the scent of life.

I'd never even seen pictures of Ireland at that age. I just knew that Ireland looked and felt like that.

I felt 'one' with nature, at peace. My heart could relax and let go of being 'on guard' at all times.

Traveling by car was also much more relaxing because there was never a set schedule or check-in at the airport. We went where the road took us.

I still travel with this philosophy today. Getting lost is the best part of the journey.

Mother Earth's energy is healing, much like that of most mothers.

The smell of cow or horse manure, even skunk spray, have always brought a smile to my face, for both scents are an indication that I am 'home', away from the busy energy of the city.

Those scenes, as well as the constant rain in Mexico City, unconsciously connected me to Ireland and Basque Country in Spain at the border with France.

I loved rainy days, and more so, torrential rain.

I've never liked using umbrellas, preferring instead to feel the cooling, cleansing sensation of rain on my face.

As a kid, I couldn't wait for the next storm so I could play in it, jumping in the puddles, carefree, honoring its force, unafraid of thunder, much like the day I was born.

Oblivious to the danger, I welcomed the roaring sounds from the heavens and the power with which they commanded attention.

Any water – rivers, lakes, oceans or rain, made me feel at home. Rain was always purifying and nurturing to me.

But, as much as I enjoyed the excitement of our weekend and summer-long road trips, I wasn't too keen on the car rides because of motion sickness and terrible migraines.

My mom's way of dealing with them was to do nothing.

She didn't think it was appropriate for a child to take pain medication, so she told me to sleep off the migraines and puke into a plastic bag if necessary.

To add to this, I was hypersensitive to heat and the sun, somewhat of an oxymoron for a Mexican.

My skin is so light that it is almost transparent, a perfect specimen for anatomy class, and the reason I've always had to be careful not to spend too much time under the sun or intense heat.

In order to prevent myself from tossing the contents of my stomach onto the back seat of my mom's Mercedes Benz, I would look out the window and focus on the moving scenery, while visualizing myself riding a white or black stallion alongside the car.

The thought of riding a horse was pacifying and empowering at the same time, distracting me from the convoluted sensations inside my belly that tried to make their way up my throat every once in a while.

Years later, I did a past life regression with Jack, one of my spiritual mentors, because I kept having recurring and vivid flashes of past-life memories about a man I had dated earlier that year and wanted to know the significance of those memories.

During the session, I traveled back in time to 1763 France.

In that life, I was married to an upper class and very wealthy, heavy-set businessman, obsessed with his business.

I recognized him immediately. He looked exactly the same, and was just as obsessed with his work in this life as he had been in that one.

He had been successful in this life, but lost everything. He blamed it on his ex, but something told me it was due to mismanagement and self-indulgence.

In 1763, we lived in a luxurious home that resembled a castle, and had four beautiful children, one of whom I recognized - my mother in this lifetime.

The marriage was a loveless marriage of convenience, as most marriages were in those times.

My husband was strictly focused on making money, and I was a decorative expectation in the eyes of society.

My children were cared for by full-time, live-in 'au pairs', as I was not permitted to be a hands-on mother because of my position in society.

As a result, I felt without purpose. I disliked the opulence in which we lived and the societal pressure to look and behave a certain way.

My husband and I disagreed over his insistence in collecting high taxes from the people who worked the land for us.

I could not understand why he had to collect so much money from them, while they struggled to feed their families. It seemed so unfair.

I lobbied for them, asking him to lower their taxes so they could have better lives, but he refused.

In rebellion, I would leave our home at sunrise and ride my horse into town to help as many people as possible, in whatever way I could.

I was an energetic healer and used herbs to make potions to help the people, and would ride back to the house late at night.

Little did I know until I did the regression session, that my mom (my daughter in that life) felt abandoned by me, not once, but every time I left the house, and again when I died.

Interestingly, my mother also dedicated herself in this lifetime to helping others less fortunate, often putting us last.

The people who worked for my husband in that lifetime appreciated my efforts and protected me from potential harm (a.k.a. the Crown).

They knew I was putting myself in great danger for defying my husband and the 'upper class', but I did not care. I could not and would not stand for injustice.

If I wasn't in town helping others, I was in the stables taking care of my horses or riding.

My obsession with horses in this lifetime was unexplainable, because I had a mild fear of them. I respected them, but knew never to underestimate their power.

As a kid, my mom took us horseback riding Western style a few times, but I hated that style of riding. It was foreign to me.

The horses were too wide, the saddles seemed awkward, my tiny legs never reached the stirrups properly, and I didn't quite have a handle of the horse while I was on it.

It felt unnatural to me.

I begged my mom for English riding classes instead, but she refused.

In early 2015, I promised myself that I would give myself everything my parents didn't provide me as a child, so I made that dream a reality.

I took a couple of dressage classes just outside of Mexico City at a renowned riding school, just to tick off another item on my bucket list.

I walked in disbelief up to a black stallion that had been assigned to me. It was an emotional moment for me. The horse was majestic. I could feel its energy from several feet away and I could tell it felt mine.

He welcomed me towards him energetically.

The instructors told me to get on the magnificent creature bareback, building momentum by following the horse as it walked, grabbing its mane, and jumping onto its back while facing forward.

It took me a few tries, but I eventually managed to get on the horse.

Once I was on it, I was instructed to ride it facing forward, then turn over so I was facing backward, and recline back until my back was completely on its back, and then flip the other way.

I felt like I was training to be in a Cirque Du Soleil production, but it was all part of the process.

If I wanted to earn the right to ride the horse on a saddle, I'd have to earn the right to do so by proving I could ride it without one.

The exercises forced me to develop a relationship with the horse; earn its trust and respect.

If I was willing to commit to training, I'd have to participate in taking care of the horses as well, brushing them, bathing and feeding them.

There were no free rides at this school. All students had to earn their place with the horses.

I had to learn to feel its energy and command it before placing a saddle on it.

After the second class, I noticed two of the instructors kept a close eye on me, a man and a woman.

I figured they were just there to make sure I didn't get too hurt.

After a few minutes, the man asked, "How many years have you been riding?"

I hesitated, "You mean, this type of horseback riding?"

"Yes."

"None, but if you count the two times I rode Western, when I couldn't even get my feet in the stirrups because the horse was too wide, and the time at 16 when the horse started galloping and I couldn't control the horse, so I fractured my tailbone…I guess only three times in my life. Why?"

"You're joking right?"

"No. Why?"

"You've never done this before?"

"No."

They both looked at each other and laughed. The woman said, "You're pulling our legs, aren't you?"

"No, why?"

"If you hadn't told us that, we would've said that you've been riding for at least 25-30 years."

"What?"

"You're a natural on a horse and if you stick with this, you'll reach dressage competitive level in no time. We're talking, six months, tops."

I was speechless.

Unfortunately, I didn't go back because of time constraints and an injury outside of class.

It wasn't until I did the past life regression session that I 'remembered' that I'd brought my horseback riding skills to this lifetime.

In 1763, horses were my only companions and confidants, which explained my love and obsession for horses in this lifetime, the peace they made me feel during long car rides, as well as my love for the French language and anything to do with France.

It was all so familiar to me.

However, in 1763, my escapes took a toll on my children, especially my mother, who was my daughter in that lifetime.

Eventually, my husband was pressured into keeping me from helping the 'poor' at all costs.

Our arguments got so bad that he wasn't willing to 'protect' me any further. His allegiance was to the Crown.

As a result, I was ambushed by soldiers on my way into town one morning. The fog was thick, the air filled with a cool mist.

My horse was spooked and I got thrown onto the ground.

Everything happened so fast, I didn't have much time to fight back.

One of the soldiers held me, while another proceeded to carry out the order.

I wasn't afraid, I'd been expecting it.

I felt the heat of a blade go into my left chest and then cut across the front of my neck.

It didn't take long for me to take my last breath.

I left the session with the awareness and wisdom of what I'd learned in the past, how my choices in that life affected this life, and the resulting soul contract I'd agreed to before incarnating once again.

I also learned that just because we feel we have a karmic connection with someone from a past life, it does not mean we need to repeat it in this lifetime.

Eureka! Soul connections need not be repeated.

Repeat after me, "Soul connections need not be repeated."

I understood he was only a test, a distraction that I was to recognize, overcome and move forward, so that's exactly what I did.

The most important thing to learn, or remember from past life regressions, is that we carry lessons forward from past lives in order to help us in our current life.

We can also go back to past lives and heal them during a regression session to stop the recurring behaviors or situations in our current life, which is something I do with clients.

A Connection to The Ocean

As a kid, I had difficulty learning how to swim, despite all the lessons I received in the all- girl British private Catholic school I attended, as well as the lessons at the local community center, and the private lessons from my mother and siblings.

My mother, an athletic woman, couldn't have been more disappointed in me.

My fear of swimming, but not of water, was difficult for her to understand because I've always loved water and being in water. What I disliked was swimming.

My school's swimming instructor couldn't get it either.

I was resistant to using my arms in the front crawl or in any swimming technique, for that matter.

She spent more time on me than any other student, but often resorted to using a pole to assist me to return to the edge of the pool.

In her words, I was a lost cause when it came to swimming.

I practiced my kicks at the edge of the pool, but couldn't coordinate my head, arms and legs at the same time when I tried to do the front crawl.

Every time I attempted it, my body filled with a trembling fear and I had to stop.

Not even the ugly white, uncomfortable rubber cap that we had to wear with our pink uniformed bathing suit helped me be a better swimmer.

"Why can't you just do as I tell you?" The swimming instructor's frustration came through loud and clear in the tone of her voice.

I shrugged my shoulders.

Eventually, I swam in my 'go to' style, which was the doggy paddle.

My report card was filled with A's across the board, except English class and Gym class.

Who fails gym class?

No one else at school struggled as much as I did in swimming class.

The girls made fun of me and wondered the same thing I wondered, *"What was wrong with me?"*

I couldn't dive or float very well either.

It was bizarre; I had no desire to swim, but loved being in water.

Then one day, the swimming instructor announced that we'd be doing aquatic ballet lessons.

All the girls jumped into the pool in their pink bathing suits.

I got into the shallow end with trepidation, holding onto the railing along the steps that led into the pool and awaited instructions.

"OK girls, float on your backs."

I let go of the railing, got on my back and floated.

Suddenly, a light bulb went on inside my head and I took a deep breath, keeping the air in, and that's when I noticed that I could stay afloat longer and higher above water if I did that.

Why had no one mentioned that before?

I was so excited that I practiced various levels of inhalation to see how much I floated with each.

My 'trick' was brilliant and I wondered if anyone else was aware of it.

I loved the sensation of the water under my body, holding me, supporting me.

The next instruction was given to extend our arms out as we floated on our backs, and sway them one way and then the other, causing our bodies to rotate in different directions.

I felt one with water, listening to its sound as I moved with it; calm, peaceful and soothing.

Then we were told to place one of our legs in a figure four and continue rotating from side to side.

Once again, I felt at home.

The instructions became gradually more difficult, but none felt foreign to me.

At the end of our class, the swimming instructor called me over to the edge of the pool.

I walked slowly in the water till I reached her.

"I don't understand. How do you go from not being able to swim to gliding like a swan in the water? It's like you were born in water. I just don't get it!"

I shrugged my shoulders and smiled with a grin from ear to ear.

This class would be a class that I would not miss for the world!

When my mom asked me what I wanted to be when I grew up, I said without question, "A marine biologist."

"Why?"

"Because I want to work with dolphins and whales and spend my life in the ocean with them."

"You realize, you'll have to learn how to swim and dive in order to do so? You can't handle being under water for very long. So, how do you suppose you'll become a marine biologist?"

I pondered on those points and realized that as much as I disliked hearing them, my mother was right.

Years later, I had a sudden random vision of being caught in a net. My body filled with anxiety. I looked down at my body while I was having the vision and realized I was a dolphin. I couldn't make my way out of the net, so I drowned.

It suddenly dawned on me that I was experiencing a past-life memory.

That vision explained my love for and connection with water, dolphins and whales.

They were my family.

It also explained my longing to be in the ocean any opportunity I could, even if I didn't know how to swim. Water was my home.

The Starseed Connection

In another session with Jack, he mentioned my Starseed origins, but I wasn't ready to delve into extra-terrestrials at the time, even though I've always believed in them.

It was just too much, too soon.

He told me to look into Arctuarian, Lyran, Pleiadian, and Syrian beings, and when I did, so much about me made total sense.

Lyran and Arctuarians believe in the Law of One. In other words, that we are one with Source energy. They operate from a place of love, light and inner peace, fairness and equality.

I was once disqualified as a job prospect after a psychological assessment showed that I'm the type of person who will sacrifice myself to ensure that others get ahead with me vs. me on my own.

True 'team' mentality was not a quality they were looking for in their organization because according to them, 'team work' is a façade in the corporate world and I wouldn't survive in their corporate culture.

It was the best compliment they could've given me.

Pleiadeans are egoless and know that the soul is a living library, or the Living Library of Akasha (also known as the Akashic Records).

Syrians are the epitome of empowerment.

Another psychic colleague told me about my Lemurian roots, and then bells went off in my head with regards to extra-terrestrials and the ocean.

It may seem strange to say that my love and fear of water were connected not just to the ocean, but also to the stars. But let me explain…

Lemurians are believed to have been a civilization of love, compassion, spirituality and benevolence. They were highly advanced and they transformed into creatures from the ocean - dolphins, whales and mermaids, when their civilization was destroyed.

I had been attracted to Lemurian and Larimar crystals for a long time, but didn't know why, until I read about Lemuria and Lemurian culture.

The root of my connection to the ocean and water was finally clear.

The 'calling' I once felt to move to Australia and visit Indonesia was also explained after finding out where Lemuria is theorized to have existed. You guessed it: somewhere between India and Australia in the Indian Ocean.

I've also always been deeply connected and attracted to the color blue, especially aqua or turquoise, which is the color of crystalline blue oceans, as well as the color of the throat chakra or the chakra of communication, where I believe true empowerment comes from.

Writing is my means of communication and power.

Lemurians were known for their connection to the healing properties and energy of water. They used their voice in the way of chanting and movement in healing rituals for themselves and others. That's what I do, I sing (in the shower) and dance in water.

Water also keeps memories. Well, everything does, but the work of Masuru Emoto in his book, *The Hidden Messages in Water* , is a great example of the power of words and their effect on water, and everything else.

Humans and all living beings are made mostly of water, including our cells.

I love meditating in water.

Lemurians were a heart-centered society that valued unconditional love, fairness, peace, Divine Feminine power and wisdom.

I know my former hesitance for swimming wasn't because of a fear of water, but rather because I didn't know how to use my limbs to help me move through the water the way the instructor wanted me to. Part of me was still a dolphin.

Instead, when I was allowed to do what came naturally to me, which was to glide and move freely, mostly without the use of my arms, I realized I loved moving through water!

After my mom applied some tough love on me during a summer vacation, I was able to overcome my fear of swimming.

She basically threw me into the deep end of a pool and walked away.

After that, she couldn't get me out of the pool.

Eventually, I gained more confidence swimming, and even started diving. I realized I was better and faster in water when I didn't use my arms, which made total sense.

The moment I let myself 'be' in water, I felt at home, twirling around, allowing my feet and legs to propel me, while my hands served to balance me or to change direction.

Water is resilient, resourceful, flexible, yet powerful and we have the qualities of water within us.

French Warrior

Another unusual interest I had as a kid was fencing. Not the type you put up around a property, but the one I watched on television, a back-and-forth dance between two masked people holding a foil, gracefully lunging at each other in an attempt to strike.

I'd watch fencing on Grandma Minnie's black and white TV after watching the Russian National Ballet.

However, instead of copying everything they did, I observed with close attention.

I never imagined how or if I would ever learn fencing, especially after all previous failed attempts to get my parents to pay for any lessons of any kind, so I appreciated the sport in silent adoration.

I became lost in the grace and versatility with which they seemed to barely touch the ground, and then they would strike one another.

It wasn't until I visited my university's sports complex in 1987 and saw the fencing team practicing, that a spark lit up inside of me.

I saw posters up on the walls advertising open tryouts for the fencing team.

This was my opportunity to see if I could finally tick another item off my bucket list.

I've always had the philosophy of trying things at least once and living my life as if I only have six months to live, so all fears about trying anything new go out the door.

Life is to be lived!

I signed up and showed up the next day at the designated time.

There was a group of about 30 students waiting in line.

They couldn't take 30 students, so they asked us to do a few steps and moves in a group. From that, they narrowed the group down to about 15 of us.

Then, they asked us to grab a uniform and get changed.

I was so excited that I did a happy dance on the spot. I was finally going to wear a fencing uniform and hold a foil.

Woohoo!

Take that, mom and dad! Ah, the feeling of independence and freedom!

I stood in line to get my uniform in a room that led into the change rooms. I was given a pair of pants, a top that somewhat resembled a restraining jacket, breast protectors and a groin guard.

I changed and walked onto a holding area when a male contender stood in front of me, scanned me from feet to head, and said, "You have a weird body."

I looked down at myself, not quite sure why he'd made that kind of comment.

Why does everyone say that? I have boobs and a round ass. How is that weird?

I spent no more than a few seconds pondering his comment, then straightened myself and tested my breast protectors by knocking on them like King Kong in front of him. I even made the King Kong sound.

I wasn't about to risk putting 'the girls' in danger.

He rolled his eyes.

Then I knocked on the groin protector just for fun.

He puffed and walked away.

I'll see you on the court douche bag!

With subtle anticipation, I stepped onto the main floor where all the potential hopefuls were gathering.

I noticed the football team practicing ballet just on the other side of the complex.

Bonus! Men in tights!

They were being cross-trained to increase their flexibility.

I have to admit that there are few things funnier than watching a bunch of tough football players doing ballet moves.

I giggled.

The fencing coach, François, had a thick French accent.

"OK, everyone. Listen up. I want you to form a line in front of me side by side and leave some room between each other."

At that moment, I was unaware that he was married to my French professor.

We followed his instructions.

"Now, I want you to follow what I do. En garde!" and he showed us step by step what to do.

We copied what he did.

He asked us to do it again and corrected some of the people in the line.

He went on to show us how to lunge forward.

We followed him as best we could.

The guy who told me I had a weird body had to be corrected a few times.

Somehow, the steps came naturally to me.

The coach asked five of us to step forward. "The rest of you can work on your steps with my assistant over there."

One of the guys in our group of five was the guy who made a comment about my body.

"Look at my feet first," our coach demonstrated some footwork.

"Now do it." He watched us with extreme focus.

"You!" he pointed at me.

I looked at the people beside me before pointing my index finger towards myself.

"Yes, *you* . Come forward."

My legs trembled a bit.

I took two slow steps forward.

I was a bit worried about being put on the spot, but since I'd gone into it with a 'nothing to lose' attitude, I had no expectations either way.

"Do that again."

I moved my feet just as he asked.

He asked me to do the step a few more times and I did as he asked each time.

He looked at me in awe. Then hesitated and finally looked around until he zoomed in on two tall guys who were practicing on their own in the distance.

They moved as if they floated, quickly, gracefully. Yet they struck each other with formidable force when they attacked.

I enjoyed watching the flowing motion of every step, the subtle, yet powerful movement of their arms, and the strength with which they lunged to strike.

They held different types of foils called sabres, which were larger and heavier.

The coach signaled them with his hand to come over.

The two guys stopped their practice, removed their face shields and walked over to us, holding their sabre in one hand and their face shield under the other arm.

Coach François introduced them to us, "Meet my top sabre players, John and Trevor. They're champions and have been training to compete in the next Olympics."

Their advanced skills showed.

"Guys, I want to see this," he said as he pointed to my feet. I wasn't sure if that was a good or bad sign.

"Do that step again," Coach François said as he looked up at me.

I was startled, hesitated for a second, and delivered.

"Did you see that?" he asked his champions.

"Impressive," they said in unison.

"How long do you think it took her to learn that step?" he asked them in his very sexy French accent.

The two looked at each other, shrugged their shoulders in perfect unison, then John said very slowly, "Five years?"

"Five minutes!" Coach François was quick to inform.

They raised their eyebrows like Siamese twins.

Coach François then turned to me, "How long do you think it took them to learn that step?"

I answered with trepidation, "I don't know…five…hours?"

"Five years!" He was quick to correct me.

I raised my eyebrows, not sure what to make of the situation.

"Congratulations!" said Trevor.

"Go back to your training," Coach François instructed them. "The rest of you can join the others over there. Gaby, you stay here."

The other four people who stood on either side of me walked away.

Coach François looked straight at me and said, "You're going to train every day with me. I will have you ready for the Olympics in six months."

I was shocked, "Me?"

"Yes, you. I've never seen anyone like you before. You have incredible potential. It's going to take hard work, but I know you'll be ready soon. You will train with me one-on-one. Can you be here tomorrow at 6:00 p.m.?"

"Yes" I said without thinking, still numb from what was happening.

"Good! See you tomorrow." He walked away to continue instructing the others.

How did a tick off a bucket list turn into an Olympic hopeful?

I had no idea how or why things went the way they did. I wasn't even sure if I had what it took to do what was expected of me. My insecurities crept up. Fear of disappointing him became stronger and stronger and my chest got tighter and tighter.

I showed up the next day a few minutes before 6:00 p.m. and changed into my uniform.

Coach François was waiting for me. "Hello, Gaby." He was wearing his fencing uniform.

"Hello."

"Let's get started."

He proceeded to instruct me on the rules, objectives, striking target areas, and purpose.

Then he showed me all the basic steps again, including how to lunge and move my arms, as well as defensive and offensive moves.

I wasn't wearing a shield yet, nor was I to hold a foil before I could prove I had mastered all the steps.

The lessons were intense.

Two hours later, we set a time for the next session.

I was in awe of how much there was to learn. I'd never been into sports. I didn't like the idea of competing, or having to work with others on a common goal. The idea terrified me.

The fear of disappointing, being put on the spot, and failure kept harping at me.

As a loner, I preferred dancing alone in my room. I didn't have to follow real people or coordinate my movements in a choreographed number.

My past instructors had been two-dimensional, inside a television. This was all so foreign to me.

I just wasn't sure if I had the commitment or discipline to stick it out. But I knew I'd give it a try.

We trained for a few consecutive days until I got the basics down.

Coach François was pleased with me, but he had one comment to make, "Gaby, in order to be great in this sport, you must be comfortable being aggressive. You must lose the fear of attacking your opponent. You're afraid of hurting your opponent. Let go of that fear. Let go of the fear of anger."

What? Me? Anger? Oh, no!

We spent considerable time practicing my attacks. We were both wearing full gear by now and practicing with foils.

"Gaby, get angry!" he raised his voice at me.

"I don't know how."

I didn't know why at the time, but I was terrified of anger. All the expressions of anger I'd witnessed growing up were of rage. Anger was not something I ever wanted to meet again, let alone feel inside of my body. The thought of becoming my grandfather terrified me.

I could see and sense the coach's frustration with me. He'd invested so much time and effort on me already and I didn't want to let him down.

The next day, I noticed he wasn't wearing his uniform. I found it odd, but didn't question it.

I guess he figured that if I wasn't going to 'attack' anytime soon, he didn't have to worry about getting hurt.

"I want you to get in touch with your anger," he said slowly, passionately, emphasizing the word, "a-n-g-e-r."

I psyched myself up and lunged, barely touching him. I was terrified of hurting him.

"Come on! You're not going to hurt me. Get a-n-g-r-y!" He raised his voice more each time he said the word, "angry."

Finally, I visualized the strike, saw myself competing in the Olympics and went into anger.

I lunged forward, extending my right arm forward with my foil in hand and lowered my left arm at the same time, striking him with just the right amount of force to make him proud.

Yes! Success was mine!

My satisfaction lasted but a second as Coach François bent over, grabbing himself between his legs.

I hadn't quite calculated where I'd strike him and certainly never imagined in a million years that I'd strike him in the groin.

The one day he didn't wear his protective gear, I had the courage to 'get in touch with my a-n-g-e-r.

I dropped the foil on the ground and ran over to him, "Oh my God! Are you OK? I'm so sorry!"

"You did fantastique Gaby! That's exactly what I wanted you to do," he said in his sexy French accent, though struggling to get the words out and unable to stand straight.

I didn't know whether to hide or die.

"You did great. I will see you here tomorrow, same time," he said.

I went into the locker room, and rather than taking my uniform with me to wash, I placed it in the laundry bin. I wouldn't be needing it again.

I also dropped out of French class. I dreaded seeing the look on his wife's face knowing that I'd left her husband without his manhood.

I spiraled into worst-case scenarios, visualizing them unable to have kids because of me, divorced because he was permanently damaged, unable to have intimacy with his wife again.

Shame took over me and I went into my cocoon. It took me a few days to even want to leave my dorm room.

How could I face the world?

It wasn't until I learned more about past lives that I understood my affinity for fencing was because I was remembering what I already knew from a past life.

I didn't have to have clarity as to the specifics of the past life, but my affinity and ease of certain activities were clear indications that I'd already learned those skills in other lives.

After this, I decided to focus my time and attention on finishing my university studies, so I could get a full-time job upon graduation.

I sometimes wish I'd had someone there to guide me, to show me that everyone makes mistakes and that one day, I'd remember that situation with humor, grace and compassion.

When I look back, I realize that no matter how many doors I chose not to walk through in life, many others opened.

Regardless of the road we choose, we eventually reach our destination, for it is not the destination, but the experiences along the way that enrich us.

Miracles In the Jungle

Throughout my teens and twenties, I had recurring dreams of waking up in a house that was on fire.

I'd open my eyes and the room I was in would be filled with smoke, but I knew the house wasn't on fire and that the smoke I was 'seeing' wasn't real. I knew it was from my dream.

To add to this, throughout my life, I was hypersensitive to heat and the sun, often experiencing sunburn from only 20 minutes of direct exposure. More than a few minutes in the sun could cause my blood pressure to drop to the point where it wouldn't register on a blood pressure monitor.

I jokingly called myself the 'walking dead'.

"You're a bad Mexican!" my friends would laugh, especially after returning from a vacation at a beach resort without a tan.

Indeed, I've never been keen on extreme temperatures, whether hot or cold, preferring temperate climates.

That smoke dream was one of my most frustrating recurring dreams, though it eventually went away.

I knew intuitively that I'd died in a fire in a past life, but had no idea how or why until I got clarity about it years later, while on a trip to Costa Rica.

I signed up for a sound healing course because I kept being drawn towards Tibetan singing bowls and quartz bowls.

I have a tendency to allow myself to be guided to whatever experiences Source (God) shows me. So, I asked Source to guide me towards the right 'teacher.'

A day later, I saw an ad on social media for a six-day Sound Resonance Immersive experience.

I was ready for a new adventure and it was close to the one-year anniversary of my mom's passing. I needed to process the wrath of conflicting emotions that went through my body during and after my mom's death.

I had also always wanted to travel to Costa Rica and this was my opportunity to tick off yet another item on my bucket list.

I fantasized about being amidst a scenery of dark rich volcanic rock and green rainforest, alongside the tranquility of the waters of the Pacific Ocean.

The location for the program was in a beautiful and peaceful self-serve retreat center in the middle of the jungle, which used to be a cacao plantation.

I'll be honest, I'd never really enjoyed having to consider someone else in my travel decisions, which is why I've always preferred to travel 'solo.'

Plus, not too many people enjoy traveling without a map or a plan. Getting lost for me is part of the magic, but for most, it can be terrifying not knowing where they're headed.

However, this adventure required me to share space with people I'd never met before, which would normally make me very uncomfortable as an introverted empath, but I was open to the idea and looking forward to a new level of growth and connection.

Less than four weeks later, I landed in San Jose and joined a group of like-minded people on an air-conditioned shuttle bus, which would take us to the retreat center.

We filled the minibus and although we didn't know each other, we began to connect seamlessly, laughing and sharing as if we'd all known each other for years.

It felt like we were on our way to an adult camp.

The driver, who didn't speak English but knew that I spoke Spanish, asked, "How long have you known each other?"

"You mean, this group of people?"

"Yes."

"Oh, we just met."

"Really?"

"Yes, why?"

"I thought you'd known each other for years. You get along so well."

I smiled.

Deep down inside, I knew that we knew each other from previous lives and we were reuniting in this one.

We stopped on the way at a tourist area that consisted of about four commercial huts, where we bought fresh coconut water and dried fruit. We also looked at clothing and souvenirs.

Just past the huts, there was a sign with a crocodile on it and an arrow pointing down.

Some of us walked over to check out the scene below.

Just over the railing, I could see the magnificent ancient creatures sunbathing by the edge of the river.

Several other members of our group joined us and expressed the same awe at the beauty beneath us. But I couldn't help thinking, *I just hope they won't be in the river that runs through the property where we're going, or make it to the ocean where we'll be swimming!*

I'd heard stories of crocodiles going into the ocean where rivers meet the sea. They were not pretty stories, but rather, worthy of a bad horror flick.

Sigh.

Breathe.

When we arrived at the retreat, we got out of the van and as I stepped out, I felt like I'd arrived 'home.'

It reminded me of all the wonderful adventures I'd lived as a child while camping with my mother.

I stood there looking around, then upwards at the lush trees, listening to the sound of the exotic birds and cicadas.

The tall arches at the entrance to the main hall in front of us had monumental figures on either side, as symbols of protection for the Mayan wisdom held within.

A Buddha rested peacefully among some vegetation, serenaded by the sounds from a variety of wild birds and peacocks on the grounds.

"Welcome," said our two male hosts, with bright smiles.

"Hello!" we responded in excitement.

Other members of the group, who'd arrived earlier, joined the welcoming committee.

I was pleasantly surprised at my calmness amidst the company of twenty complete strangers, which in the past, would have felt incredibly uncomfortable. But this trip was about discovery, whatever that may be, and so be it.

I was open to 'just being,' judgment-free.

The location was even more magical than in the promotional videos.

The energy was fabulous and the sound of cicadas electrified the field around us unlike anything I'd ever witnessed.

I laughed when other members of the group spotted poop on our path to the cabins, noting that the property must have cats, then screamed when they noticed dragon sized iguanas climbing up the palm trees nearby.

Ah, home.

I dropped off my luggage, which consisted of a backpack. I like to travel light.

In my years of traveling, I'd learned to carry the essentials in my carry-on, which included toothbrush, toothpaste, flip flops, towel and bikini, should the airline decide to give my luggage a worldwide tour at their cost.

As it turned out, my other bag had taken such a tour.

I changed into my bathing suit and headed out to explore.

The rooms were rustic. The property was filled with all types of fauna, including beautiful toucans, colorful peacocks, iguanas, hummingbirds, dragon flies, cicadas, bats, rather large spiders and more.

I loved that there was basic electricity, but no TV or radio, room service, laundry or housekeeping service, and no Wi-Fi except in the main hall where we were to gather for our delicious and filling vegan meals three times per day.

In the side yard, you could relax by a calming pool, surrounded by fragrant trees and a canopy of blue skies.

The scent of a strong, yet tantalizing aroma could be perceived in the air, which drew me closer towards the pool, where I came face to face with the most magnificent tree.

I said, "hello" to it and its splendid flowers, the color of linen and sunshine.

"What kind of tree is this?" I asked one of the people I could see just inside the kitchen.

I assumed she was preparing lunch for the group.

"Ylang-ylang."

"Wow!" I picked up one of the flowers that lay on the ground below and brought it close to my nose with delicate care.

I used Ylang-ylang essential oil in healing sessions with clients, but I'd never actually had the pleasure of being this close to the actual flower.

She was more magical than I'd ever expected! The essential oils do not do her justice.

After lunch, we were given an official tour of the property, where they focused on each of the types of trees and vegetation that made the plantation so special: cacao, cinnamon, and passion fruit, as well as the local wildlife.

All I could focus on was taking deep breaths and being grateful for the experience, feeling my mother's presence beside me through it all.

We were lucky that we were there during the dry season, because it rains pretty much every day the rest of the year.

The concept of the retreat center was more like going glamping than staying in a hotel, and it was exactly what I'd been looking for.

I walked up the stairs to the open-air mezzanine above the main building and looked at the grounds below from this vantage point.

I could see the river in the distance and the pool below me. The cicadas continued serenading us.

The mezzanine floor also had a private yoga and meditation studio.

I walked in to get a feel for the energy in the room, and when I turned my head to the left, I saw a massive butterfly painted on the wall.

Tears began to flow down my cheeks. I knew it was my mom's way of letting me know that she was there supporting me, and to allow myself the freedom to experience life to the fullest, just as she had always done.

I no longer felt a false sense of responsibility for others. I could focus on me, for a change.

Our days started with a wake-up call from nature at exactly 5 a.m., when the cicadas began singing. They stopped their symphonies at precisely 5 p.m., like military trained soldiers.

Each day around 7 a.m., Stefan, the lead facilitator, would gather the guests from one cabin and everyone from that cabin would play enchanting and angelic sounds with various musical instruments around the other cabins. The next day, another group would take a turn doing our wake-up ritual, and so forth.

It was like being woken up with the soothing sounds of forest fairies.

After the very first wake-up call, I couldn't wait for the next morning. Every day the rituals would bring us to a higher level of bliss, as we became one with nature.

Afterwards, the group would walk back to their cabins and get ready for the day.

At 8:00 a.m., everyone would meet just below the main hall on the yoga platform overlooking the river, where we saluted the sun for about a half hour.

This was followed by a walk down some stairs that led to the river, where we paid reverence to Pachamama, and connected with the cleansing and loving energy of water.

We would then gather together on the rocks to listen to Stefan talk.

One morning, when he began to share his wisdom with us, I saw a kayaker pass by on the water behind him in a yellow and orange kayak.

I was surprised because not only was it an unexpected sight, but it also brought back vivid memories of my mother kayaking on a river in Mexico when we were kids.

I was enchanted by the view and my eyes began to fill with tears. This was no coincidence.

I could feel my mom's presence more and more as the days passed.

Thank you.

After connecting with Mother Earth by the river, we walked back up to the main hall for an energizing vegan breakfast, but not before giving thanks to Pachamama for the much needed nourishment we were about to receive.

Although I'd always resisted saying grace at the dinner table, somehow paying respect to Mother Nature seemed natural.

Our days were filled with wisdom from our facilitators. We learned beautiful and interesting teachings about the history and healing power of sound, as well as the unique vibrational frequencies of each of the instruments and the materials with which they were made: chimes, tuning forks, drums, spirit drums, gongs, Tibetan metal singing bowls, quartz bowls, kalimba, bells and especially the human voice.

The classes were also healing. We experienced first-hand the effects of sound resonance, which was often complemented with meditation, and sometimes yoga.

We took a break for lunch, thanked Mother Earth before our meal, and continued learning in the afternoon as we detoxed our bodies mentally, physically, emotionally and energetically.

The afternoon sessions incorporated facilitation exercises to open our hearts further.

The pre-dinner ritual was similar to the one we did before the morning and afternoon meals. Everyone took turns saying a prayer of gratitude to Mother Earth for her blessings.

Evenings gave us a chance to break the rhythm of our daytime rituals, connecting us to divine energy with ecstatic dances and cacao ceremonies, where we were free to express ourselves without rules, judgment or fear, through movement and sound.

On the first night, we did a burning fire release exercise, where we wrote down all the emotions, memories and thoughts we wanted to let go of, all those things which no longer served us, and threw them into the fire.

Then we chose whether or not we wanted to share what we released with our soul brothers and sisters.

The ritual was raw, cathartic, meaningful and emotional for all.

Every day brought me closer and closer to my higher self, to my guides and to the purity of unconditional love with these strangers and myself.

There were no expectations, demands, or pretenses.

How could this be? How could I feel so connected to people I didn't know? Me, the person who didn't let strangers in?

That's the magic of removing ourselves from everyday 'things to do lists' that we wear like an invisibility cloak, which only serve to distract us from what's really important in life, which is 'being' and 'connection' vs. 'doing'.

When we're surrounded by the sanctuary of Mother Earth, we can easily give ourselves permission to be our authentic selves, physically, mentally, emotionally and spiritually, naked and unapologetically.

I've learned that people will judge us no matter what, so why not be judged for being our authentic selves?

Mother Earth's energy is also one of the most healing frequencies that exists.

It was then that I understood why retreats are so successful and why often, rehab facilities are set up in isolated areas.

Every morning, before our wake-up ritual, I'd hear an angelic sound coming from the river.

It was a voice unlike any other I'd ever had the pleasure of listening to.

She reached notes that few are able to reach, and I never wanted her to stop, especially because she blended so well with the chimes of our morning rise-up fairies.

After the third day, I realized that 'the celestial voice' belonged to one of my soul sisters in the group, Laurie, a professional singer.

"Please don't ever stop!" I said with gratitude at breakfast before we sat down.

"Thank you!" she smiled.

I seemed to be tuning into her energy more so than others and saw flashes of one of the past lives in which we knew each other.

During lunch she overheard me explaining to the people at my table that even though I'm a Reiki Master, I don't believe that we need symbols to do energy medicine.

I say this with confidence because I've practiced energy medicine since 1987, and having done much research and learned various techniques, I know that all techniques work on different levels.

The most important aspect of energy medicine is intention, belief and trance state.

Laurie, however, disagreed with me, "You're insulting Reiki Masters!"

"Really?"

"Yes."

"OK, let me ask you this: let's say I have a piece of wood and I want to drive a nail into it. Can I use a hammer to do it?"

"Of course."

"Can I use the back of my shoe?"

"Yes."

"Can I use a stapler or a rock?"

"Yes."

"All those tools, no matter how different, will eventually work. Energy medicine is no different."

"I'd never looked at it that way."

I smiled.

After that, Laurie and I developed a deep respect for each other, our powers, and our stories.

On the fourth day, I decided to take part in a temazcal ceremony, despite every bone in my body saying, "No."

I wanted to challenge myself in an unusual way and at the same time, face one of my worst fears.

I followed the group to a part of the plantation where the permanent structural frame of the temazcal was located.

The ceremony would be carried out by a local shaman, who carefully prepared the ground, placed the blankets on top, lit the fire for the stones and prepared the herbs that would be burned in the ceremony.

We were told to wear our bathing suits or be naked because it would get really hot inside.

I asked some of the members of the group, who'd done a sweat lodge ceremony in the past, what it was like.

"Hot."

Great!

We waited what seemed to be hours until the temazcal was ready for us to go in.

I wore my bathing suit and brought a wet wrap with me in case I needed to protect my nostrils while inside.

Before we went in, I made sure I drenched myself and my wrap in cold water again.

Each of us was shown the way to enter, crawling around the center of the temazcal, where the hot stones would be placed in a hole on the ground.

We were directed to make our way to the opposite side of the temazcal, forming a U.

We were told how to sit, how far from the stones, and what to do if we experienced a negative reaction during the ceremony.

"You must fight your inner demons. Every part of you is going to want to rush out, but you must fight the urge to run. Face your fears. It's not uncommon to experience emotional releases during the ceremony. Become one with the heat of the fire."

I became more and more hesitant.

"If you absolutely must leave, know that you won't be able to leave until one of the doors opens."

There was only one door as far as I could see, but what he meant was that the door would open four times in total throughout the ceremony to allow some of the heat to escape, and in relation to the four elements of the ritual.

I also didn't know that it took at least twenty minutes for each of the doors to open.

The heated stones, each representing an aspect of nature, were placed in the center of the temazcal, in a hole that had been dug in the ground.

I could feel the heat coming off the stones. I tried to remain calm through this phase by focusing on my breathing.

Water was poured onto the stones and the steam began to rise.

I was sitting two places away from the door, but on the opposite end, meaning I was the second person to enter and hence, the second last person to leave.

Clearly, I hadn't done one of these ceremonies before and had no idea what I'd gotten myself into.

I thought I had strategically chosen a spot close to the exit, just in case I had to make a mad rush for fresh air, but what I selected instead, was the furthest place.

There are no coincidences.

I felt the heat from the stones become more and more intense as water was added.

I tried to talk myself through the fears. I closed my eyes, but the heat burned the inside of my nostrils.

I bent forward, getting as close to the ground as I could, and grabbed the wrap I'd brought with me, using it to cover my nose and eyes. It helped a bit.

I felt like I was going to suffocate and faint. I had no idea how much time had transpired, but I knew I had to get out of there or I would die.

Suddenly, I began to have flashbacks of the past life where I'd died in a fire.

The visions were more vivid, as if I was reliving the experience.

I panicked.

I could feel my heart beat faster and faster. My chest felt tight. I couldn't breathe. I started to shed tears of desperation.

"I need to leave!"

"You cannot leave. Fight your fears."

"No, you don't understand, I'm going to die!"

"No, you won't."

"Yes, I am!" I started making my way toward the exit on my right.

"You cannot leave now! You must wait until the door opens!" the shaman said.

"I have to go now!" I yelled back in tears.

"If you leave, you must leave from this side."

I tried to make my way over the stones.

"No! You must honor Mother Earth and this ritual by crawling all the way around the stones and leave from this side."

I couldn't believe he was being so difficult.

Could he not sense the medical emergency that was about to happen if I didn't leave?

I should've known better than to have participated in the first place, but it was too late for 'should haves.'

"Do it slowly," he said sternly.

"Fuck!" I crawled slowly until I made it to the exit.

When I was finally out, I gasped for a breath of life.

Once I got my bearings, I sat down on a log and wept uncontrollably until the second door opened.

As I did, more clarity came to me about my connection to that past life.

Moments later, when the second door opened, another person left, a French man, who was also angry. He almost jumped out.

I was surprised at his desertion because he seemed to love the heat, but sweat lodges aren't for everyone.

The experience was enough to convince me that I would never put myself through any heated experiences ever again. I finally understood why I stay away from golf, hot yoga, hot tubs, saunas, steam rooms, or exercising outdoors.

There are some challenges that don't need to be experienced.

Despite the difficulty, I was grateful for the insight into that past life, as well as my courage and willingness to face my fears head on.

On the second last afternoon of the immersive, we were asked to lay on the mezzanine floor for a meditation and sound bath.

I placed my yoga mat close to the railing that overlooked the pool. It was late afternoon, so the cicadas were still singing with synchronized precision, though their humming did not overpower the sound of the bowls, as Stefan played and sang.

I lay on the floor with my eyes closed, free of expectations, completely open to all possibilities, as the sound vibrations reached my body.

I began to see a kaleidoscope of colors in my mind, and then a beautiful big, bright white light, through which I could see and sense the energy of the most beautiful female angel descending upon me.

I'd never really come across such an extraordinary being this way before, so unexpected, unsummoned, unintended.

She was tall and floated parallel to me, just above my body, facing me.

I felt peace, just like the peace I'd felt on that glorious day inside that chapel in Mexico City a few years prior.

Her eyes were blue and brilliant, her hair white and luminescent. Her entire body radiated white light.

She looked exactly the way that Pleiadeans are described.

The sense that I got from her energy was pure and unconditional love.

I was in complete awe.

She extended her right hand and penetrated my abdomen at the same level as my liver on the right side, as if reaching for something, then pulled her hand away very gently.

I could tell she'd removed something from my body.

I couldn't get a sense of what it was, but I knew with complete certainty that she was there to heal me.

I communicated with her telepathically.

I don't know what you just removed, but thank you. Thank you for my healing.

She smiled back at me and without saying a word, levitated above me and disappeared.

I felt tears running down the side of my face.

I wasn't sure what I'd done again to deserve this miracle, but I was grateful for it.

Keep the miracles coming. Thank you, thank you, thank you!

On our last night before we were to depart, we sat in a circle on the yard surrounded by Ylang-ylang trees.

The fragrance of those magnificent trees gently reminded us of the beauty of Mother Earth and I gave thanks for all my senses.

We faced each other in the circle. Each person was given a quartz bowl with a striker, which they held in front of them.

I sat beside Michel, Stefan's assistant, eager to begin playing because the entire week I tried to play the bowls, but none would play for me.

I wasn't sure why, but I was beginning to wonder if the bowls didn't like me.

As silly as it sounds, I believe that we must develop a relationship with our tools, whatever they may be.

The mosquitoes were fierce. Everyone kept applying commercial mosquito repellent, but it wasn't effective against jungle insects.

My friend Randy, an experienced traveler, had warned me against jungle bugs. "Make your own and bring it with you because Deet is not effective against jungle mosquitoes."

He was right. I pulled out my homemade repellent made with a variety of essential oils and sprayed it on myself.

It worked like magic.

Once I was able to shield myself from the swarming pests, I refocused on the singing bowl in front of me.

I was trying to communicate with the bowl, trying to understand why I was the only person in the group who couldn't get a bowl to play.

Everyone took their strikers and began to test the sound of their bowls.

I struck mine and a dull sound came from it. I tried again and ran the striker along the rim of the bowl to encourage the bowl to sing, but there was no sound.

I tried again and again, but nothing happened.

Frustrated, I asked Source telepathically, "Why won't it play for me?"

I got the answer immediately, "Just observe."

"Why? I want to play," I contested.

"Put the striker down and observe. Just be."

I pouted like a child, but did as instructed.

By now, everyone was playing their bowls with beautiful cohesion and synchronicity.

Stefan, who was leading the melodies, asked, "Who wants to be the first to lie in the center of the circle and experience the effects of a sound bath?"

One of the women in the group raised her hand. He signaled her to go ahead.

She put her striker down, got up and gently lay down on the grass, extending her arms and legs like a star.

By now, the skies were illuminated only by the beauty of moonlight and stars. The only other light around us was a dim glow from the main building, giving us just enough light to see each other.

As I watched her lie down on the grass, Spirit guided me to look at the bowls.

I began to notice the energy from each of the bowls spill over, like white smoke from a cauldron, hovering ever so gently over the surface of the grass and into the center of the circle, bathing the woman on the ground.

I closed my eyes and rubbed them to make sure I wasn't hallucinating.

While keeping my focus on the marvelous spectacle before me, I leaned over to Michel and asked, "Are you able to see energy?"

"No, why?"

"Oh my God! If you could see what I'm seeing right now!"

"Really?"

"Yes!"

Another person took a turn in the center of the circle.

I observed the magic in total and complete wonderment.

I became so excited that I couldn't contain myself any longer, so I asked the group, "Can anyone else here see energy the way I do?"

Everyone responded in unison, "No, why?"

"If you guys could see what I can see!" And I described to them what I was witnessing.

"That's amazing!" said the woman beside me.

Stefan looked surprised, even though he'd demonstrated to us the effects of the bowls on water.

I let go of the inner conflict I'd created trying to force sound out of the bowl in front of me, and relaxed instead, while I continued to take in the miraculous magic.

Thank you, God! Thank you!

The next day, I was sad that we had to part ways. This was not a typical end of vacation feeling for me.

I always enjoy vacations, but can't wait to get back to my home base. Not this time.

As I arrived at the airport, I longed for a reunion with my soul sisters and brothers, knowing I'd miss the moments we'd shared.

I got on the plane for the flight home with a renewed sense of being, empowered and ready to live life with a transformed perspective.

Halfway through the flight, however, the plane began to shake from side to side with increased levels of intensity until it shook violently.

Then it moved up and down and side to side again.

I'd been through turbulence many times in my life, having traveled extensively over the years, so it wasn't something that typically scared me.

However, this was one of the worst cases of turbulence I'd ever been through.

The pilot came on the speaker, "Ladies and gentlemen, we have a bit of a rough ride ahead of us, so I ask that you please remain seated until the seatbelt lights have been turned off."

The plane shook like a tin can full of pennies.

Being prone to motion sickness, I'm not fond of turbulence, but manage to remain calm through it most times.

If I had to give it a level of intensity on a 1 to 10 scale, the turbulence was a 9.5.

The only level 10 turbulence I'd experienced was while taking off from Las Vegas airport as crosswinds hit the plane and the wings swayed from side to side, almost touching the ground.

My usual way of dealing with turbulence is falling asleep and hoping to wake up when it's all over, but this was not typical turbulence by any means.

I couldn't fall asleep while we were being shaken violently every which way.

The overhead compartments popped open and people's belongings began to fall out.

At first, I thought there wasn't anything that could be done about it, except try to remain calm, but then a bell went off in my head.

Everything is energy. Everything. I can change this.

So, I closed my eyes and visualized a tree deeply rooted into Mother Earth that grew high enough to cradle the plane in its branches to keep it steady.

The moment I did this, the turbulence stopped. Just like that. When I became tired, lost focus or started dozing off, the turbulence started again.

I re-focused, visualized the tree again and the turbulence stopped.

I tried to take my focus off the visualization a few times, but each time, the plane began to shake.

So, I decided to sacrifice my beauty sleep for a Zen flight.

It worked.

About an hour later, the pilot came on the loudspeaker and announced that it was safe to take off our seat belts.

Right after I arrived home from Costa Rica, I wrote the group a note that read:

Dear sisters and brothers from another mister:

Writing is the path of my soul. It is the way in which I express myself best, so I thought I'd send you this before we reintegrate back into our lives and forget:

Six Days

Six days and a lifetime of memories imprinted so deep in the essence of my soul, replacing old wounds, patterns, and negative remnants of times past.

Six days of pure joy, encouragement, emotions, learning, support, sharing, healing, compassion, admiration, respect, freedom, vulnerability, trust, truth, passion, connection, reciprocity, inspiration, gratitude, and most importantly, love.

Six days was all it took to prove that regardless of our differences, we are one.

Six days, which started with strangers, that like concrete struck with a beam of light, surrendered into fine sand, only to become a beautiful sculpture emanating peace, love, light, and a healing sound that unites us into eternity.

Six days to transform the meaning of the words, "Are you happy?" into a smile.

Six days to fill my heart with joy upon hearing the word, "cacao."

Six days to turn running water and breaking waves into cleansing love.

Six days for the sensation of the sun's rays against my skin to become warmth in my heart.

Six days to convert an early morning wake-up ritual into a longing.

Six days to give every meal divine meaning.

Six days to transform "thank you" into a lifetime of gratitude.

"You should write this shit down!" you said.

I do.

May your lives be forever filled with loving rituals as you return to the Source.

Thank you, Stefan and Michel, may the Source be with you. XO

Love, Gaby

I wrote Stefan a separate note:

Connection is one of the most fundamental of human needs.

The sound resonance retreat established a safe space for that connection to occur, allowing me to reconnect with my soul, inspiring me, freeing me, touching me, and allowing me to return to unconditional self-love.

It invited me to dig deep, release, and love myself and everything around me from a different perspective, genuinely and authentically.

It allowed me to expose the beauty of my soul at its best, raw, unapologetic and real.

Every day was a gift. Every meal, a reverence. Every morning, a delightful ritual.

I learned more than how to make beautiful sounds that heal your spirit.

I learned to create and incorporate loving rituals into my daily existence.

To say that it was life-changing, doesn't begin to express what an incredible journey this was for me.

Definitely not your average workshop, not your average facilitator, not your average anything. Every moment, every detail was conscious, flowing and loving.

Thank you for your guidance, teachings, inspiration and unconditional love.

Love, Light and Healing Sound,

Gaby

...

A week later, I was on another trip, on my way to San Jose, California when I saw the angel once again, and she was just as magical as before.

A few days after returning from that trip, I remembered getting the results of an ultrasound I'd had done a few months prior to going on the trip to Costa Rica.

My doctor had given me the not-so-great news, "Well, it looks like you have non-alcoholic fatty liver disease."

"I have what?"

"I know. You don't drink, so it doesn't make sense, but you know how you keep saying you're going to lose the 35 lbs. of extra weight you've gained?"

"Yes."

"Well, it's time to start losing instead of just talking about it. I want you at no more than 125 lbs."

"You're worse than a controlling boyfriend."

She laughed.

I went for walks, stopped eating out as often, and reduced my portions.

Three weeks after the trips, I went for a follow-up ultrasound and my liver was one hundred percent healthy again.

Then I remembered the white angels in Costa Rica and California, and smiled.

...

I hope that these stories have awakened a curiosity in you about your own DNA or past-life memories and the reasons why you may have unexplainable interests or skills without having learned them in this lifetime.

Now, I'll introduce you to some stories that changed my beliefs about life and death.

Reflection Time:

Think back to when you were a child. Did you speak of other places or people in such a way that they seemed familiar to you?

Have you ever longed for places, food or things without explanation as to why?

Do you ever travel to locations for the first time that feel familiar, like you've been there before?

The Miracle of Eternal Life

March 14, 2005, I went into a church out of respect for my grandmother.

It was her funeral.

Her passing was one of the biggest and most difficult losses I've ever experienced.

She'd always been my pillar of strength and refuge, but it was now time for me to maneuver through life on my own two feet.

Throughout my life, I called her once a week on Sundays to hear about her life and family drama, and she'd always want to hear all about my life.

She was the family matriarch and the one everyone turned to for financial and other types of support.

I didn't care about her generosity. She was my best friend and I loved hearing her voice. It gave me comfort. She made me feel loved unconditionally.

It took everything I had to keep my emotions under control during the time that she was in hospital prior to her passing.

I had no choice. I couldn't let her see me crumbling on the inside. She was a strong woman and a great mentor. Her devotion to her family could never be questioned. I wasn't about to let her down. I had to be there for her the same way she was there for me.

My dad had called me two weeks prior to say, "I think you better come say 'good-bye' to your grandmother."

My father was also a psychic medium, so I knew if he was making the suggestion, I better go.

I was in a relationship with a wonderful man at the time, but his family was toxic and his inability to set boundaries with them put a tremendous strain on our relationship.

We were on the brink of shattering. His lack of support towards me going to Mexico to say goodbye to my dying grandmother put us over the edge. His coldness about her illness and his inability to see how important she was to me and how much I needed to be with her, showed me that he was not someone I wanted to share my life with.

Even though we were engaged and had just bought a house together, I ended the relationship before I left for Mexico City.

I stayed by my grandmother's side for two weeks, taking showers in the hospital, using the wall as a pillow, surviving on vending machine coffee and street vendor food, but none of that mattered.

I didn't even consider it a sacrifice. There is no sacrifice in love. My grandmother would have done that for me and more. She already had.

Those two weeks were a rollercoaster of hope and fear, sadness and acceptance, laughter and grief, knowing all along that she wouldn't leave the hospital.

It wasn't a question of *if*, but rather, *when* she'd pass.

We met with a gerontologist, who told us how important it was for her not to be immobile, and how easily the elderly become depressed and deteriorate in institutional settings.

Next was a death and dying specialist, who offered her insight on the process of dying, what to expect and how to support her in the process, as well as surgeons who gave us a prognosis.

I was well aware of the phases of death. I knew the short-term improvements were part of the process.

I had to be strong for her. She was there for me as a child, when no one else wanted me. She showed me the unconditional love that no one else considered important, proving to me that there was at least one person on the planet who could smother me with hugs, kisses, caresses and the words, "Te amo."

Grandma Minnie made sure I knew that I mattered, that I was heard and seen. I wanted to do the same for her.

I wanted the honor of holding her hand as she transitioned, or as she called it, "changed address."

As I placed my head on her bed just beside her legs, I watched her lay there, her chest rising and sinking slowly, then resting. I sensed her gather her strength as she struggled to keep herself from dwindling away.

My mind drifted to the memories of wiping her kisses off my face.

"Don't you like my kisses?" she'd ask to express her disappointment in my behavior.

"Ew, no!" I'd answer, frowning. I've never been very good at lessening the blow of truth.

It wasn't the kiss I disliked, but the technique, the slobbery saliva full of germs she left on my cheeks, which I felt the need to wipe off immediately.

To say that I was hyper aware of germs was an understatement.

My thoughts drifted back to memories of when I would place my head on her lap as a child, and even as an adult, so that she would caress my head. As she did, she'd sing lullabies to me.

I didn't have the heart to tell her that her singing voice made my skin cringe more than the screeching sound of a nail on a blackboard. So I'd lift my hand and gently closed her lips.

"Don't you like my singing?"

"Just hum," I'd say with a smile.

And she would, followed by, "Te amo. Te amo tanto."

The memories brought gentle tears to my eyes and a smile to my soul.

I lifted my head a little, so I could get a better look at her fragile hands resting on the mattress.

The age spots decorating her skin highlighted the wisdom within.

A couple of years earlier, I'd asked her what it was like to be her age.

"On the inside, I feel nineteen, but my body reminds me I'm not," she said with her signature smile.

Suddenly, I felt her hand touch my head, a subtle reminder that she was there for me, even in her final hours, and to be in the moment.

I was grateful.

She instilled the art of living in the moment after making many trips to India. She loved India and Japan and had great respect for Eastern philosophies and beliefs.

From the age of three, I watched her do yoga and meditation every morning, but not before going for a two kilometer speed walk in the neighborhood at 5 a.m.

I copied everything she did, laughing at the fire breath during yoga, and when I was old enough, I joined her in her walks.

Those small, seemingly insignificant moments with her were the memories that impacted my life more so than her generous gifts.

I actually had to tell her that just because I said I liked something in a store, it didn't mean I wanted it, and it most certainly didn't mean that she should buy it for me.

"But if you like it, I want you to have it!"

"Grandma, I can admire the beauty in things without having them."

"OK," she'd say and then ask where I wanted to go for lunch, which was always our favorite restaurant, Los Vegetarianos, in downtown Mexico City.

Her kindness and compassion molded part of who I am today.

The days and nights transpired in slow motion, as if buying us time. Family and friends made their rounds visiting. Most had hopes that she'd recover, but I knew better.

We'd gather in the hospital cafeteria, laughing and crying together.

Even on her deathbed, she was able to bring the family together, if only one last time.

One of her doctors, Dr. Mendez, was particularly kind to her, and I was very grateful to him.

I smiled every time I saw him walk in the door. He made me feel safe in the midst of the inevitable.

My grandmother would move her eyes as if to say, "he's over there, go say 'hi'…" but I felt guilty even thinking of paying attention to a man while she was dying.

Her mind was deteriorating as well as her body. When the doctors checked on her, she'd signal them to get closer to her and then she'd slap them or swear at them, "Pendejo!"

I didn't know whether to laugh, cry or both, or whether to hide from embarrassment, but compassion took over. I was well trained by her.

She began hallucinating, "Jesus is standing in the corner," she said.

I wasn't sure if it was Jesus or not, but I knew her guides were showing up to let her know she was not alone. They were patiently waiting for her to make her transition.

On my grandma's last night, my stepmother forced me to go to my dad's. "You need to take a break," she said, as she led me out of my grandmother's room, down the elevator and into a cab to make sure I wasn't going to change my mind.

It was 9:30 p.m. I arrived at my father's, took a warm shower, ate a healthy meal and looked forward to sleeping on a bed for the first time in two weeks. I fell asleep as soon as my head touched the pillow.

Looking back, I believe it was my grandmother's way of protecting me.

The phone rang at 3:30 a.m.

I woke up immediately.

It's amazing how our bodies and mind become hypersensitive in tense situations to help us manage in the best ways possible.

I've always said that if there's ever an emergency, you want me in charge.

I heard my stepmother's steps making their way to my room. She opened the door and delivered the inevitable news, "She just passed."

My heart cracked, but couldn't crumble. There were still so many things that needed to be taken care of.

We rushed back to the hospital.

My dad talked to the nurses and doctor in the hallway. They were processing the documentation we'd need for the funeral home and transporting of her body.

I took that time to say 'goodbye' to her.

I walked into her room with trepidation, as if unwilling to disturb her.

I'd seen dead people before at funerals, but none had been anyone close to me.

I always commented how 'good' people looked in a coffin. The care that went into preparing the body was evident.

To my surprise, Grandma Minnie's body had already been wrapped like mummy.

That was fast!

I assumed it was to prevent the body from stiffening in awkward positions during rigor mortis.

What a peculiar protocol to wrap people in such similar ways when they're born and when they die.

I placed my hands gently over her feet at the end of the bed, "Te amo. Te amo tanto."

My dad and I headed to the funeral home to make the final arrangements.

We chose a simple casket for the viewing and an even simpler urn for her ashes.

The viewing was scheduled for 9 a.m. that morning.

We went back to my father's house and got ready for the hours that followed.

The funeral home filled with a blend of tears and uncontrollable laughter, just like our family gatherings.

If there's something Mexicans are good at, and my family even better at, it is finding humor in the darkest moments.

Grandma Minnie's lifeless body looked so different in a casket.

I wasn't impressed with the way they'd done her makeup, but kept quiet.

Seeing her in the casket made me appreciate the true meaning of life. It is our soul that matters, not the physical body.

We took our seats in preparation for the service.

The priest walked into the room and began his sermon. His words seemed like a muffled sound that filled the air.

I began to feel the armor of strength that I'd worn for the past two weeks begin to lift, exposing my vulnerability.

I looked around at all the faces in the room. I knew everyone, but they were empty faces to me.

The words I was hearing were void of meaning.

The room began to spin.

I felt my chest fill with pressure until my heart finally crumbled.

The release of tears was uncontrollable, like water violently hitting rocks in a fast-moving river.

I got up from my seat and walked out of the room, unable to resist the explosion of convoluted emotions in my body.

The sensations moving through and out of me were freeing and unbearably painful at the same time, much like giving birth.

Grandma Minnie was cremated at 5 p.m.

I stayed with friends at their weekend home in Cuernavaca, an hour away from Mexico City, for a couple of days to decompress.

My common-law partner had communicated with me via e-mail only once during the two weeks. Nothing had changed between us, so I assured him that I'd be back as soon as I could in order to begin the process of separating assets.

The thought of returning to Canada to put an end to another sad, yet inevitable chapter in my life was not as tragic as what I'd just gone through.

I felt good about the future, as uncertain as it was.

I set myself free upon my return to Canada and took refuge in work. I've always said that the longest marriage I've ever had was with my work.

My commute to work was 45 minutes each way, which prior to my grandmother's passing, seemed like forever to a type-A personality like myself.

However, those 45 minutes suddenly became a sanctuary of peace, especially as I became aware of my grandmother's presence in the car with me.

Her spirit sat beside me on the passenger side and I felt her so strongly, that I could almost 'see' her.

I felt her watching me, smiling at me, caressing me. The sensations were so strong that I started talking to her out loud in the car.

At first, I questioned those conversations. I wondered if it wasn't wishful thinking.

Was it all in my head? Was it a coping mechanism? How could I know for sure?

I didn't care. The conversations became my little secret. I spoke to her every day on the way to and from work.

"You knew I'd end things with him, didn't you?"

"Yes. Sweetheart, you deserved more. He's a good man, but you deserve to be in a family that loves you, with an emotionally mature man, who would stand up for you and protect you if necessary."

"I just don't know if I'll ever find someone like him ever again."

I didn't realize that I was forming a limiting belief with that statement, nor that it would take me close to twenty years to break.

We talked about everything, including our experiences and memories together, as well as the issues and decisions I faced at work.

I felt guilty about not spending more time with her when she was alive, but she reassured me to let go of the guilt.

At the same time, I enjoyed the benefits of her being fully in spirit form.

I no longer had to call her, but missed the action of calling her.

I no longer had to wonder where or how she was or what she was doing because she was beside me at all times.

I could smell her perfume and breath, but she wasn't there. It was bizarre.

There were so many opposites, but I didn't care. I was going to take what I could get and learn to adapt.

I was overwhelmed with joy at the thought that she was there all the time.

Nevertheless, I cried every day for three years after she passed.

My grandmother had been my rock, my ally, my best friend and my sanctuary.

I dealt with my grief by rowing every morning for 20 minutes, and repeated the routine in the evenings, crying the entire time.

I also cried on the way to work. Her presence, though comforting, triggered me.

It wasn't long before I travelled to Mexico again. The company I worked for needed someone to conduct a market research project, and they selected me for the job.

Soon after arriving, my stepmother suggested I accompany her to see a local psychic.

I jumped at the opportunity.

I had taken two weeks off before I was supposed to start my new assignment. I used it to get more acquainted with the ways of the land, and rented an apartment within walking distance of my father's house.

The psychic's office was located on the second floor of an older building in an established area of Mexico City.

We made our way through Mexico City traffic and arrived early for our appointment.

The waiting room looked like a doctor's office, with grey fabric chairs lined up along the walls and in rows in the center of the room.

There were at least 15 clients patiently awaiting their consultation.

I guess you could say he was a doctor, but of a different kind.

I couldn't believe that a psychic could be so busy every day and work so many hours.

The wait was long. Several hours long.

As a type-A personality, I was not a patient person, and just as I was about to say, "Let's go," to my stepmother, my name was called.

His assistant showed me into his office. "Please wait. He'll be right in."

There was a large window along the back wall.

It was nice to see natural light coming in.

The desk was full of tacky multi-colored trinkets, photographs and other personal items.

The old-fashioned brown bookcase behind the office chair was adorned with similar objects.

There was a faint scent of incense in the room that reminded me of Grandma Minnie's house.

He walked into the room wearing an outfit similar to something that Liberace would wear. "Hello my dear. My name is Luis. I don't believe we've met before."

"No." I was amused and curious at the same time, with zero expectations.

He sat down across from me on the other side of his desk.

"You recently experienced a huge loss, didn't you?"

Was my face that obvious?

"Yes."

"It's an older woman, like a mother figure to you. She watches over you."

Could he be more generic?

He went on to say a few more things about the older woman who'd just passed and he must've noticed the look on my face that said, "unimpressed" because he then said, "You don't believe I'm telling the truth."

"Well, it's all a bit generic."

His demeanor changed. He adjusted his posture, sat up straight, almost as if I'd just challenged Liberace to play the piano. He continued,

"You only have one photograph on display in your entire apartment and it's of your grandmother."

I raised my eyebrows. He had my attention.

"She used to call you, 'My little princess'."

Tears released from my eyes and flowed down like a broken faucet. I reached for a tissue from the box on his desk.

"You talk to her every day on the way to and from work. In fact, you can feel her right now. She's here with us."

"Yes," I smiled.

I wasn't crazy!

He went on to tell me all the messages my grandmother had for me, all of which validated my ability to communicate with her.

That validation gave me the self-confidence I needed to trust what I knew, and stop questioning myself whenever I felt a spirit near me and/or talking to me.

…

My grandmother's passing was an important transition for me as well. Not only did I have to learn to survive without her moral support, but her passing awakened my gift of communication with souls, which I elaborate on in the next chapter.

Reflection Time:

Have you ever sensed the spirits of your loved ones around you after they passed?

If so, how does it make you feel to sense them?

Does it give you a comforting feeling to know that they never leave our side, even if you don't feel them?

Do you feel comfortable talking to them? If not, what prevents you from doing so?

The Miracle of Communication

My practice using my intuitive and healing abilities has always been unique, and my clients more so.

After Grandma Minnie's passing and realizing I could talk to dead people, a Pandora's box opened up.

I began to sense spirits coming through, especially during Reiki treatments.

The first one was with a client who'd recently lost her husband. She'd been by his side the entire time he was sick and needed a little TLC after he passed.

I was glad she came to see me because I could sense the grief in her energetic field, as well as the stress oozing out of her body.

She had mentioned how stressful the past two weeks had been, especially dealing with her husband's children from his first marriage.

Halfway through the treatment, orbs of light suddenly appeared out of nowhere. They were everywhere above her body and to the sides.

They were beautiful, a light golden color, and looked larger than fireflies flying around.

The client had her eyes closed, so she was unaware of what was happening.

I wondered for a moment if this was an 'aura' prior to a migraine for me.

Was I going to have a seizure or drop dead? If I did, this would be a great 'last vision' to have before dying.

But I soon realized it wasn't anything so dramatic.

It was her husband's spirit.

Telepathically, he gave me the messages that I was to deliver to his wife.

"Please let my wife know that everything is going to be OK. I know she didn't marry me for my money. Tell her not to let my kids intimidate her. She's going to be fine."

It was my first time having to relay messages for someone and I wasn't quite sure how do it, especially because this client had come to me for treatment for the very first time. She didn't know me well, and we hadn't established enough trust or rapport for me to relay that type of message.

So, I began to go back and forth in my head with his spirit, "Ah, I can't say that. Your wife doesn't know me from Jack, and I can't just suddenly say to a total stranger, 'Oh by the way, your dead husband, you know, the one you just took care of for the past two weeks at the hospital before he died, is talking to you through me,' without her thinking I'm completely insane."

"Just find a way to say it," he said.

"Find a way?"

"Yes," he said.

I said nothing to his wife, who was still enjoying her treatment on the table, for what seemed an eternity as I tried to figure out what to say to her and how to say it.

Finally, I had enough courage to say, "You know, even though you've been through a lot in the past two weeks, I think your husband would want you to know that everything is going to be OK. No matter what his kids and family have said to you, he knows the truth. You married him for love and he knows that."

She kept her eyes closed, but tears began to run down the sides of her face, "You have no idea how much I needed to hear that."

I felt a huge sense of relief, satisfaction and gratitude as I smiled.

At that moment, the orbs disappeared and I felt his presence leave.

Mission accomplished.

I thanked his spirit for the honor of allowing me to speak for him.

Later that month, I booked an appointment with Jack, my tough-love spiritual mentor.

"How do I know I'm not making things up in my head?" I asked perplexed.

"Easy! Ask your guides for validation!" he said in an authoritative tone.

"What kind of validation?" I asked, still unsure of what he was leading to.

"Ask them for symbols that could only mean something to their loved ones, or ask them for their names," he clarified.

"I can do that?"

"Yes! You keep telling people that you don't know who's talking to you, but you do know!"

"No, I don't," I said defensively.

"Yes, you do. Start asking them."

"OK."

"The sooner you surrender, the sooner things will start to flow. Stop fighting your path!"

"OK." I finally raised my energetic white flag.

He was tough, but I was used to tough. My mother was a tough-love person.

A few weeks later, I was about to start a Reiki session with a client.

I wasn't sure how the session would go because I sensed her energy from afar and knew she was in a very negative space.

I had been told by a friend of hers that she was going through a tough divorce.

When she got on the table, I thought, *oh boy* …

I didn't want to work on her, but she was there and I couldn't just walk out.

I figured it was a test from Source.

She had been told about my gifts, so I knew she wasn't going to think I was crazy when I started talking.

I sensed a spirit come through. I couldn't see it, but felt it.

"Tell her she doesn't need her love."

I became confused.

"I thought she was married to a man. Why are you referring to a 'her' when you say that?"

"Just tell her."

I relayed the message. The client didn't look impressed, "My grandmother used to say that."

"I have no idea if it is your grandmother or not. All I see is an older lady's smile, but not the full face."

"Tell her she doesn't need Anyka's love," the spirit said.

Anyka? Is that even a name? That sounds Russian. I don't think this lady is Russian.

"Just tell her!"

My rebellious nature wouldn't give in. "Can I ask you, what nationality are you?"

"I'm from Czech Republic. Why?"

"Well, spirit is saying that you don't need Anyka's love. Do you know any Anykas?"

"I know a lot of Anykas," she said sternly.

Great! You couldn't give me a more generic name? I need specifics!

"Ask her who Anykat is."

Anykat? You better be right!

"Do you know an Anykat?"

She looked even less impressed than she did before, "I know a lot of Anykats."

Great! You're killing me here!

"Ask her who Yuri is," the spirit instructed.

Yuri?

"Yes!" the spirit said.

"Who is Yuri?"

The client's eyes widened.

Then, very slowly, they filled with tears until she couldn't contain them anymore.

"I know exactly who you're talking about."

Phew! Bingo!

"This spirit wants you to know that you've lived your whole life seeking validation from others and you have to stop. You're going to be OK. You're stronger than you've ever given yourself credit. You're going to find the strength within to inspire others in the future. You need to trust that everything will be OK."

"My grandmother used to say those things to me all the time."

I sighed. "It's probably her. I couldn't make this shit up if I tried."

I finished the treatment.

The client stood up and looked at me as she said, "I'm going to tell you something, so you can understand. Anykat is my best friend back home. Her name is Anyka, but I call her Anykat as a pet name. She's been my rock during my separation, but she's sick and I don't know what I'll do without her. Her son's name is Yuri."

"Thank you for explaining because for a moment, I wasn't sure if you were having an affair with a woman. None of it made sense to me, but as long as it makes sense to you, that's all that matters."

"Thank you. Now I know you're the real thing."

I smiled.

"Can I give you a hug?" she asked.

"Yes, of course!"

"I feel so much better now. Thank you."

And just like that, I felt her energy shift, as if a massive load of bricks had been lifted off her.

I thanked her grandmother's spirit for coming through and guiding me in the process.

A couple of months later, I went back to see Jack, my tough-love spiritual consultant.

"Why do you keep fighting your path so much?"

"I don't know."

In retrospect, I was just afraid to let people down. I was also afraid of judgement, but I've come a long way since then. Not only have I embraced my path and purpose, but I'm so confident in my gifts that other people's opinions or judgements don't affect me in the least.

I've had people call me a fraud, a crazy woman and worse, but I know that as long as I stay on path and continue serving, the opinions of others are just a 'test.'

I've also realized that my job is just to be a messenger and not to get in the way of the messages by trying to make sense of them.

When I'm unable to tap into someone's energy field to read them, it's because I'm not meant to be their reader. I'm not supposed to be the one delivering the message for them.

It is also not for me to control the outcome, only to relay the message. After all, each person has the gift of free will and freedom of choice, and those choices will bring them either closer of further away from their goals.

Each choice we make can also switch us from one parallel to another, and all possibilities of outcomes exist at the same time. There is no such thing as 'getting it wrong,' just different choices.

There is also no short-cut to awareness, a.k.a. remembering. Each of us must go through the path in the way we choose.

Being a medium is not about me. My job is to be the voice for spirits and facilitate the communication between souls and the living. I like to think that I'm a cell phone between the souls of the living and the souls of those who transitioned out of human form.

Every day that I do what I do, I am grateful for my gifts. It is a privilege to speak for souls.

But, communication with the souls of the departed isn't the only type of communication that exists. We can also communicate with Source energy, our higher selves and other spirit guides.

...

The next chapter goes into more detail as to how you can manifest miracles into your life.

Reflection Time:
Have you ever seen or sensed spirits around you?
Have you ever heard them, either in your head or actual voices?
If so, how did you feel when you became aware that it was happening?
Did you answer back? If not, what holds you back? Is it fear or doubt?

The Miracle of Awareness and Manifestation

It may be easy to assume that when you've been aware of your psychic abilities your whole life, you also have clarity about the way things are and how they work from a spiritual perspective, but that's not always the case.

We are able to read ourselves, but our emotions often block or distort the messages. Also, lack of self-confidence can test the best of us until we develop ways to validate our intuition.

Anyone who says, "If psychics could read themselves, they'd win the lottery!" didn't meet my father. He won the lottery in Mexico twice. The numbers would come to him in dreams.

Many psychics, empaths and the like, can operate from a place of fear, and our individual trauma and perspective of life will affect our development and reading style.

Awakening journeys can seem like a boat at sea without a sense of direction. Sometimes they go towards the horizon, and sometimes they go in circles.

I first came across the trilogy of *Conversations with God* by Neale Donald Walsch in 2007, after searching in the self-help book section of my local bookstore for something that could answer many of my questions about life and spirituality.

So, I set the intention to find the answers because I felt an inner yearning to 'know' more and explain why I've always felt so 'different.'

Guess what happens when you start seeking? The Universe delivers.

The bookstore, which was called Chapters at the time, had a novel format: you could grab a book and sample read it before you bought it.

I loved that store!

I came across Book One of the *Conversations with God* trilogy on display on a center island.

It got my attention, so I picked it up and read the introduction.

Neale Donald Walsch had me at, "…You're about to have a conversation with God…"

How did he know I already spoke with God?

I wasn't able to put the book down, so I walked over to the cash register, paid for the jewel I held in my hands and went home to continue my intimate encounter with this wonderful treasure I'd just discovered.

I couldn't believe that I'd finally come across someone who 'got me,' who understood that each of us can have open and candid conversations with the Creator, Source, or God.

After all, I'd had conversations with God since I was a child.

As soon as books two and three came out, I devoured them with the same passion as I had book one.

The trilogy contained every possible question anyone could ask God, and the answers that came to Neale on paper.

This, by the way, is also the gift of automatic writing, where you ask the question and wait for the answer to come.

Yes. It's that simple.

Then came, *The Secret* , which was a movie gifted to me by a co-worker.

At first, I didn't know what to make of his gift, until I watched the movie.

Finally! Something that explained how I was able to tune into a Universal 'knowing' and 'trusting' that I would buy a car, get a job, or meet someone.

It was called the Law of Attraction!

What *The Secret* did for me, was put a bit of a structure to my manifestation abilities, as well as help me snap out of negative thinking patterns and focus on the positive, so I could attract more of it.

It was so simple: Ask, Believe, Receive, Gratitude.

In case you're wondering, all of the manifestation techniques that have become known in the past twenty years are all based on the work of Jose Silva in The Silva Method, which my Great Aunt Toni taught me so many years ago, but I hadn't paid enough attention to, likely because I wasn't ready for the lessons then.

With the Law of Attraction, I manifested a luxury lakeview condo at Marina Del Rey in Toronto, my first official business, the car I wanted, and everything else since!

I remembered driving by that condo in 1992 and thinking that it was so far from my reach to live there, but I had this 'knowing' that I would live there one day.

Fifteen years later, there I was!

I'd forgotten Toni's teachings that 'our focus creates our reality.'

When I was reminded of The Law of Attraction after watching *The Secret*, I used it to the most, and everything I ever wanted began materializing even more so than before.

In 2007, I also decided to leave the corporate world and transition into healthcare, not knowing if I could do it, or how, but I set the intention to do it, and did it.

I designed and printed my business cards before graduating from the program and saw myself owning my own clinic.

Within a year and five months, I had achieved all of it.

That same year I read, *The Power of Intention*, by Wayne Dyer and again found someone else who 'got me.'

At the start of the book, Wayne Dyer asks the readers to skip to "Chapter 15: A Portrait of a Person Connected to the Field of Intention", before you read the rest of the book.

I did just that, but had to put the book down for a moment afterwards so I could allow myself a full-on emotional release.

Wayne Dyer had just described me as if he'd profiled me in his book.

Then I watched the movie, *What the Bleep Do We Know?* which went into the Law of Attraction from a slightly different perspective.

I continued reading as many books as I could get my hands on, slowly putting the pieces of the puzzle together.

I also spoke with mentors, other psychic mediums, about their own experiences, only to realize that each of our paths is so unique, you cannot possibly try to compare your life with that of others.

We're not meant to have the same teachers or experiences. Each of us is drawn to the teachers that are right for us at the time, and as soon as we learn those lessons, we'll move onto the next, and so forth.

Some of the lessons may resonate and some will not. The important thing is to be open to learning, free of judgement, and take what we want out of them. Our spiritual development never stops.

I had just read the book, *E2* by Pam Grout in 2013, in which she encourages the reader to do a series of exercises to prove that God exists.

This was a new way of learning how to manifest, including setting a deadline. I thought I'd give it a try, as I'm always open to new techniques.

There was a set of materials that I had to get for the experiments, so I decided I'd buy them towards the end of the day.

In the meantime, I wrote down what I wanted to manifest that day, as per her instructions.

I wanted to see butterflies before the end of the day, but not just any kind of butterfly, they had to be purple butterflies.

It was the middle of August, and it had been raining for about two weeks non-stop in Toronto.

I knew that it would be next to impossible to see a butterfly on a rainy day, let alone a purple one.

The challenge was given and it was up to God to deliver.

Once I finished writing down the challenge, I watched TV in hopes of catching a butterfly on screen, but nothing appeared that resembled a butterfly.

4 p.m. came along and I figured I should get to the local dollar store to get my supplies before they closed at 5 p.m.

I drove to the store slowly, hoping to catch a butterfly printed on a wall, a car, anything. But the roads were gloomy and greyish, and everything else on the way seemed to match the weather.

Once inside the dollar store, I got distracted by all the goodies. I drifted from isle to isle aimlessly as if I had fallen into a trance state.

I walked around and looked at almost every item in every isle, which I don't usually do.

My modus operandi is to go in knowing what I'm looking for, get it and leave. If there's something I don't enjoy, it is wasting time 'shopping'.

It wasn't until I reached the gardening section that I remembered what I'd gone to the dollar store for, and laughed inside.

I looked up at the wall in front of me and thought, 'Oh yes…wire, cotton balls, and…' I took out my shopping list because I couldn't remember the next item on the list.

That's when a little voice in my head said, "Turn around."

"Why? I need to find these items. I've wasted so much time already."

"Turn around."

"No. I need to focus."

"Just turn around."

Reluctantly, I turned around to face the items behind me.

I was speechless.

Before me was an entire wall of purple butterflies.

I didn't need proof that there was a God, but it was fun getting validation this way.

In my head, I said, "Oh, wow! You're good, *really* good!"

Then I smiled and looked down at my list.

I couldn't wait to get home to work on the other exercises.

Today, I have a few purple butterflies in my office to remind me of God's power, and as a reminder that I can ask for specific signs to validate a situation, or as an answer to a question.

Every book and/or movie on manifestation has a similar message.

Some authors claim to have a better formula for manifesting, but they all essentially got their information from others before them.

I like to keep my manifestation mojo calibrated by manifesting small stuff almost daily, like finding a parking spot that is most convenient for me.

An example of these small manifestations is when I chose to manifest new age music.

After years of listening to the same CDs over and over again, I'd grown tired of them and wanted new material to listen to, but didn't want to spend a fortune on CDs.

I said, "Universe, I want new age music CDs, but I want them for FREE, so do whatever you need to do to get to me pronto!"

Yes. I command the Universe.

Then I went about my week, trusting that the Universe *would* deliver.

The following weekend, an acquaintance who runs a natural health product multi-level marketing company asked me to cover for her at a bridal show.

I said, "Sure." I didn't really have anything else to do and I love working tradeshows, so I figured, *why not*?

She'd also asked another person, a young up- and-coming actor, to work the show with me, so we could support each other.

When I met the young man, I said, "You're going to do very well in your acting career."

"Really?"

"Yes. Your work ethic is amazing and it will pay off."

"Thank you!"

By the way, several years later, he's consistently getting hired for acting gigs and I know he's on his way to stardom .

I decided to walk around the room for a bit and I stopped at a real estate agent's booth.

We chit-chatted a bit. She seemed super friendly and promised to drop by our booth as soon as she got a chance.

I went back to my booth and continued working until about an hour prior to closing, when the real estate agent came by.

"Hey! I just wanted to let you know that I have a couple of boxes full of music CDs that I don't want to take back to the office with me, so please feel free to drop by and take what you like."

It never dawned on me to ask about the genre of music, so a few minutes before closing, I dropped by her booth again, and looked in the boxes.

They were filled with hundreds of new age CDs.

I smiled from ear to ear and chose ten CDs.

"Take more!" she said.

"How on earth did you end up with these boxes?" I asked.

"My partner and I used to work for a CD distribution company. When they went under, we kept boxes and boxes of CDs. Are you sure you don't want more? I'm not taking them back with me."

"Oh, I'm good with these, thank you so much!"

"If you change your mind, I'll be here for a bit after the show."

"OK, thank you again."

"My pleasure! You're actually doing me a favor!"

I went to my car and said to the Universe, "You always deliver! Thank you!"

A few months later, I was looking for furniture and trinkets to decorate my new place, which I'd also manifested in one of my favorite areas of the city, and close to work.

I said, "Universe, you know the style of sofas I like. I want a new or fairly new sofa for free or next to free."

The next day, I was scrolling down a used goods website and came across what I thought said, "Designer sofa for sale."

I wasn't too sure if I should click on it because of the 'designer' part, but did anyway.

The lady selling it said that her sister had tried to clean the sofa with bleach and accidentally stained it, but it was in perfect shape otherwise.

They wanted it gone because they were down-sizing and wouldn't be needing it anymore.

I went to see the sofa right away and upon inspection, realized that the bleach stain was subtle and not visible, unless you were looking for it.

It also came with a sofa chair, an ottoman, and a 6'x 8' carpet.

Total price for all items: $120.

You better believe I said, "Thank you!"

I paid more for the rental of the moving truck and the pizza and beer for the friends who helped me move.

A few days later, I said, "Universe, remember those metal chimes I had at my old house, which I absolutely loved and regretted giving away when I moved? Well, I'd like to find them again at a second-hand store, so do what you need to do. Work your magic and again, and remember, I want them next to free!"

Two days later, I walked into a local thrift store, and as I made my way up and down the isles I saw a small version of the chimes I had asked for. They were wrought iron with bells in the shape of a rhombus.

I picked them up right away and placed them in my cart. "Thank you!" I said, "Now, I don't mean to be ungrateful or anything, but do you think that the next time, I could find the original, larger size of these?" and I laughed.

The manifestation goes even further though.

There was a time in Mexico City when I was feeling low and had almost no money to my name. I believe I had the equivalent of two dollars in my pocket for food till the end of the month.

I was struggling financially, but I was too proud to ask for help. My father could have given me money or food, but I wanted to get out of it on my own.

I took my dog for a walk and put the money in my pocket so I could stop at a convenience store to buy myself something to eat.

However, when I got there, I realized I'd dropped the money along the way.

I was devastated. I had no money to buy food.

I went home, cried and asked the typical, "Why?"

The next day, I took my dog out for his morning walk, and a little voice in my head suggested I look down.

"Why?" I asked.

"Just look down."

I did and to my surprise, I found the equivalent to five dollars on the ground. I looked around to see if I could find the person who'd dropped it, but there was no one around.

I understood then how powerful and compassionate God is. I couldn't contain the tears that gathered in my eyes, so I surrendered and let them flow.

Shortly after that, I started doing better financially.

This was absolute proof to me that Source energy and our guides are always there for us, constantly conspiring *for* us, and all we have to do is get out of our own way and trust.

Faith requires blind trust.

The other important thing I've learned is that when we don't get what we want, it is because there's always something better waiting for us. Remember the following, "Rejection is God's Protection."

Lastly, I'm going to give you a Master's Degree in Manifestation in ten words or less with the following phrase:

"Universe, make it happen and show me the way!"

The first part of this phrase, "Universe, make it happen," is where you step into your Divine power. The second part, "Show me the way," is where you surrender to Divine intervention and timing.

The Universe loves balance. All opposites exist in the Universe. You cannot be weak and not strong. You cannot be powerful and not vulnerable, light and not dark, nice and not a bitch, giving and not allow yourself to receive, a leader and not a follower.

This is also known as the concept of non-duality. Every opposite imaginable exists in the Universe and you and your body (mental, emotional, physical and energetic) are part of the Universe.

By stepping into your power and then trusting in the Universe to deliver, magic happens.

I teach this to clients and they usually come back with, "It works!"

One client used it at a mall during the Holiday season and she wrote me to tell me that she had set the intention to win a contest that was going on while she was at the mall, and guess what happened?

She won the contest! She was so happy and then started using it on everything else she could think of.

The important thing is that she had fun with it and let go of fear.

...

In the next chapter, I discuss the importance of forgiveness for your own personal growth. Repressed emotions block our spiritual development, so it's important to understand that our reluctance to let go of emotions that don't serve us anymore only anchors us in the past and takes our attention away from our connection with Source energy. They also lead to dis-ease in the body.

Reflection Time:

Have you ever tried manifesting?

If so, how did it go for you?

Have you ever missed out on something, an opportunity, a purchase or person, only to realize that something better was waiting for you afterwards?

How do you practice gratitude?

Do you practice gratitude only when good things happen or do you include the lessons?

After reading this story, what will you have the courage to step into your power and manifest that you've been wanting for a while?

The Miracle of Forgiveness

I was lying awake one night around 3 a.m. in the spring of 2013, in Mexico City.

My mind was overwhelmed with a whirlpool of thoughts about my failing relationship, business, my health, and the ailing health of my father and stepmother.

Suddenly, I noticed that an acquaintance of mine, also a psychic medium, was online on a social media platform.

We messaged back and forth for a bit, and then she said, "By the way, your grandfather is here."

I immediately assumed it was my paternal grandfather, "Oh, that's nice! Is he short, bald with white hair?"

"Actually, no. He's tall, darker skin and dark green glasses."

I knew immediately it was my maternal grandfather, Victor.

My body tightened up like a concrete wall. "What the hell does he want?"

She was quick to respond, "He wants to say he's sorry for all the harm he caused you and the entire family when he was alive. He knows the reason your lives are the way they are is because of his abusive behavior. He says he was a monster in life."

I paused.

"Yes, he was." I took a moment before I continued. I was so reluctant to have that conversation with him. I never ever expected him to make contact with me after he passed. "Look, if it's going to help his soul somehow, then fine. He's forgiven, but the damage is done and unless he can do something to undo it, forgiveness means nothing. If he wants to do something about it, he better help his daughters because they're completely fucked up."

"He wants you to relay this message to his whole family. He's really sorry for his abusive behavior and all the damage he caused."

"Look, the intention is nice, but I haven't had any contact with my mother or her family for over 11 years, and I'd like to keep it that way. That family is beyond toxic."

"You have to do this for him!" she pressed.

"I don't have to do a thing, especially for him! You have no idea what kind of a man he was. When he says he was a monster, he's not understating it!"

Suddenly, memories of times forgotten began to resurface like a backed-up toilet about to overflow.

He beat us every opportunity he could.

I saw him slap my mother across the face when she questioned why she wasn't allowed to go on a date with a suitor, even though she was divorced.

He forced us to eat rotten food.

To say he was abusive put it mildly.

"You have to do this for him!" she pressed on.

"Look, I appreciate what you're trying to do, but I'm not going to do a thing. If he wants help, he's going to have to find another way of getting the message to his family because I'm not doing it! This conversation is over."

"OK, but just know it's your duty to do as he asks."

I thanked her for the message, and politely ended the conversation.

I was so angry afterwards that it took me weeks to get over it.

I kept going over the conversation in my head day after day, trying to make peace with my feelings and beliefs about the choices I'd made up till then to stay away from my mother and her family.

Self-preservation, sanity and peace of mind were my priorities, and I wasn't going to go back on that just because my grandfather decided to come through.

It took me a couple of years to come to terms with his request. When I did, I tried to find my mother and her siblings, but had no luck.

I had no idea how to find her.

I figured it was meant to be, and just as well.

I doubted that she'd believe me if I told her that her father had apologized for being so violent.

She always defended him and denied he was every physical with her, her siblings, or us.

Years later, during a session with Jack, my grandfather Victor came through again.

I felt him come through that time, but I'd let go of the anger by then. Emotions tend to block our perceptive abilities.

"Your grandfather is one of your guides, did you know that?" Jack said.

"I had a feeling he was hanging around," I said.

"He wasn't a good man when he was alive, was he?"

"Not at all, but apparently, he wants to make up for what he did, and if that's the case, so be it."

A few months later, I was doing a reading with a client at a psychic fair, when I felt him come through.

The client was also a psychic medium. I had seen her come into the room and knew she'd end up at my booth eventually.

She approached me and asked if she could have a reading.

"Sure, but you're way stronger than I am. You can actually see spirits, so can I ask you, why do you want a reading with me?"

"I haven't been able to connect with my guides for a while and have no idea why. I'm stuck," she said.

"OK. Let me see what comes through." I did my ritual for establishing 'connection' and began to speak.

Everything I said was validated by her, as she sat across from me.

Suddenly, she felt the need to interrupt me, "Please stop. You need to stop."

"OK. What's going on?"

"I'm sorry, but I've never experienced anything like this before."

I smiled and turned my head like a puppy.

"Do you know who your guides are?"

"Yes. One is my grandmother, another is my grandfather, and…"

She interrupted again, "Do you know where your grandfather is standing right now?"

"Yes, just behind me to the side. Why?"

"Well, like I've said. I've never experienced this before and it's distracting, bizarre! Just before you speak, your grandfather tells you what to say and you repeat it a second afterwards. I can hear spirits just as I hear you, so it sounds like an echoing effect. He literally tells you what to say and you repeat it verbatim."

I smiled, "That's very cool! I always tell clients that I couldn't make this shit up even if I tried. I'm creative, but I'm not that good. It doesn't come from me."

"No, it doesn't!"

"Well, I guess you know now with one hundred percent certainty that I'm not making this up."

"No, you're not. You're the real deal." She smiled.

I smiled back and as I did, I felt an entourage of spirits line up to the side of my booth.

She turned her head slightly towards the display table and began to cry.

"Your spirit guides are here," I said.

"Yes. They are," she said as tears ran down her face.

I handed her a tissue, "I can't see them, but I feel them."

"They're all here. I don't know how to thank you."

"You just needed to go through this in order to unblock yourself. You're very gifted, but you've been under so much stress lately that it blocked you. It happens to the best of us."

We both got up from our chairs and hugged.

"You're so wonderful, thank you," she said.

"So are you. Thank you for your trust and thank you for validating what I do and say."

She left with an immense sense of gratitude.

I sat down and thanked my grandfather. "I guess we're a team now. Let's do this."

I've been working with him ever since, though he's not my only guide. I too, have an entourage, and so do you.

I tell clients to let go of any grudges with their loved ones or anyone who hurt them because it doesn't mean that they will continue to hurt them in the afterlife.

The human experience doesn't mean that we will be a reflection of that in spirit form.

Be open and willing to let go of the past.

Forgiveness doesn't mean you have to excuse what happened, but rather, that it no longer has power over you. You can take your power back.

An acquaintance was devastated because her family had taken her male cousin's side when she finally had the courage to speak up about his abuse towards her when they were kids.

To this day, they refuse to believe her.

She will not move on until she gets an apology from him and from her family for not believing her.

My question to her was, "What if your cousin dies? What if he's unable to say 'sorry' to you? What if he's incapable because he doesn't have the skills or mental capacity to recognize that what he did was wrong? Will you give him and your family all your power by holding onto the idea that they must apologize before you can heal?"

Trauma doesn't have to stop us from moving forward.

We can take our power back by looking at situations from a different perspective.

Had I held onto the past, my grandfather perhaps wouldn't have become one of my greatest helpers.

Being aware that even though he hurt so many people, he is redeeming himself by helping me now, and that is healing. It is also one of the most loving experiences I could have dreamed of, and better than an apology.

...

In the next chapter, we're going to explore the other side of the cycle of life, The Miracle of Conception and how I was able to witness it first hand from an energetic perspective.

Reflection Time:
Take a sheet of paper and draw a line down the middle.

On the left-hand side, write down a list of all the people who've hurt or disappointed you.

On the right-hand side, write down the following beside each name:

"Even though you hurt me by_____, and made me feel _____, your actions and behaviors no longer have power over me. I release the effects and take my power back."

When you've completed this exercise, take a moment to reflect on how this feels for you.

If you feel lighter, congratulations!

If you feel reluctance or resistance, visualize yourself placing the sheet of paper in a hot air balloon and releasing it until it reaches the sun and disintegrates.

Take ten deep breaths and give thanks for the ability to release that which no longer serves you.

The Miracle of Conception

It was the autumn of 2013. I'd been casually dating a guy in Mexico City who, let's just say, had a hard time understanding the concept of 'monogamy,' so I wasn't planning a future with him.

After a night together, he left and I searched for a movie on TV to watch, but nothing was interesting enough for me to want to stay up, so I shut off the light and tried to fall asleep.

Although I lay there motionless in the midst of darkness, my mind kept trying to come up with the best way to break the news to him that our fling had reached its expiration date.

Suddenly, out of nowhere, I saw an orb of light move towards me.

It was a beautiful bright golden color, similar to the orbs I'd seen when my client's husband came through for her during a Reiki session.

It moved around slowly in different directions: up and down, and side to side.

I was fascinated by it and for a moment, I thought I might be dreaming or hallucinating, so I shook my head.

I was fully awake.

I sat up a bit, keeping my focus on the orb.

Then it took a sudden turn and headed closer to me.

I wasn't sure what it was going to do, so I kept observing it. Suddenly, it took a dive into my womb.

I felt it go through my lower abdomen into my uterus.

At that moment, I had a sense, a 'knowing', that I was pregnant.

I was in complete awe of how miraculous conception really is.

I tried not to think of it and said nothing to anyone for the next five weeks.

I wanted it to have been a dream because the possibility of being pregnant by that guy was not an option. He was the last person on the planet I'd want to have a child with.

A few weeks later, I realized I'd missed my period, but that wasn't uncommon for me. I'd always had irregular periods. I didn't want to freak out, but every cell in my body said, "Oh no!"

I'd been told by my doctor many years prior that it would be almost impossible for me to become pregnant and that if I ever conceived, I would most certainly be unable to keep the pregnancy.

She was correct. This wasn't be my first pregnancy.

The next day, I walked to the local pharmacy and purchased a pregnancy test.

I went home and waited till the next morning as per the instructions.

I got up early and went to the washroom, placed the test under my urine stream, put the cap back on, and waited a few minutes.

I hesitated to grab the test after the time was up. Every part of me wanted it to be a false alarm, just another irregular period for me.

I couldn't wait any longer. The curiosity was getting the best of me.

I turned the test over and looked at the little bars on the screen: *positive* .

God, not with him! Anyone else but him, please!

I wanted it to be a bad dream.

I wasted no time and booked an appointment with my gynecologist the next day to do a blood test, in hopes that the urine test had been a false positive.

I was in my early forties and the last thing I needed was a high-risk pregnancy.

I kept telling myself, "I'm too old...I'm single...I can't have kids..."

The gynecologist gave me the requisition form to take to the lab downstairs.

I went down to the lab and had my blood drawn.

As I waited for the results, I felt changes happening in my uterus.

I could feel something was wrong, so I went to the washroom.

I was bleeding. I knew what that meant and felt a huge sense of relief and sadness as I felt the energy orb leave my womb.

I went back to the waiting room.

The lab's receptionist handed me the results in an envelope.

I didn't want to wait to get back to the doctor's office, so I opened up the envelope right away.

The results read: *positive*.

But I knew I was no longer pregnant. It wasn't my first miscarriage.

Every inch of my body felt cold. The Universe had answered my pleas.

I walked back up to my doctor's office and handed her the results.

"You better check me. I'm bleeding," I said.

She hurried me into her office.

I placed my feet on the stirrups at the end of the examination table and spread my legs open.

She felt my abdomen and then examined me internally.

"You're in the midst of a miscarriage. We'll have to wait until tomorrow to see if your uterus expels everything on its own or if I'll have to do a DNC."

"OK," I said.

I got off the table and got dressed.

The gynecologist lectured me before I left her office, "Please, don't get pregnant again. I'm not sure if you're trying to get pregnant or if this was an accident, but I'm not saying it because of the risk of Down Syndrome. That's the least of your worries. At your age, the probability of dying during childbirth is exponentially higher. If you want children, adopt."

"OK."

I drove to the home of the guy I was having a fling with to give him the bad news/good news. His face showed a smile of relief, which validated what came out of my mouth next. "We're done."

"What do you mean?"

I walked out and didn't see him again.

When I got home, I wept alone until I couldn't cry anymore.

My eyes were swollen, my face was red, and my body felt weak.

I had miscarried physically, emotionally, mentally and spiritually.

All those years of wondering if I'd ever meet Mr. Right and have a happy family had finally culminated into a tough resolution: any chances of having a family of my own were now gone.

The conflicting emotions were bittersweet.

On one side, my biological clock had never done a tick tock inside of me. On the other, I knew I would have made an amazing mother, but not everyone is meant to be a parent.

In the middle of that flurry of emotions, I found enough calmness to be grateful for the miracle that I'd witnessed.

It made me realize that a soul goes into a fetus at the moment of conception, regardless of all the theories from 'so-called' experts in the spirituality field, who had differing opinions as to when a soul enters the body.

I'd seen it with my own eyes and felt it in my body.

Losing that last pregnancy made me realize what a miracle we are and how fragile life can be.

I named my unborn children Alexandra Isabella (second pregnancy) and Christian Patrick (first pregnancy). I know their spirits are with me at all times.

...

The next chapter deals with another difficult moment in my life, which proved to me just how strong I am and that unconditional love has no boundaries: my mom's transition.

Reflection Time:

Have you ever had a feeling that someone around you was pregnant before they told you the news?

If you've ever been pregnant, did you feel energetically different? What non-physical signs led you to the realization?

If you've had the misfortune of experiencing the loss of unborn children, do you ever feel their spirits around you?

Do you feel that they may have incarnated into someone else or a pet?

If so, how does this make you feel?

The Miracle of Unconditional Love

My mom passed in early 2018.

The last memory I had of her was of an argument. I'd given her an ultimatum, "We either go to family therapy or you never see me again."

Her response was stern, "I'll never go to therapy".

I never understood her reluctance. I believe that she may have had a distrust of psychologists because of her involvement with Scientology. I also believe that she was terrified of being vulnerable, or potentially diagnosed.

"Then, I guess this is goodbye," I said.

She was in denial, "You won't even come to my funeral?"

"No." I walked out the door and never saw her again.

She left me no other choice. Being in contact with her exposed me to physical danger through my brother's violent episodes, as well as financial, mental and emotional abuse.

I had to choose between my mental, physical health and emotional health, and my need to feel close to my mother.

I chose me. I had to look after me or no one else would.

I cried every day for three years after I walked out that door.

No amount of therapy could take away the pain, but I was proud of myself for having the courage to walk away from a toxic cycle of deception and abuse.

My mom, through no fault of her own, had learned to lie in order to protect herself from her father's abuse.

I understood the effects of her own trauma, as well as the efforts she'd made to overcome it, change her own patterns and guide us to avoid repeating them.

"There's no need to yell," she'd say.

Her intentions were good, but the cycles kept repeating over and over again.

Breaking negative cycles requires tremendous courage and hard work. It is painful and difficult to navigate through, but necessary.

I hadn't seen my mother for over 18 years prior to getting a call from her first cousin, Aunt Lucy, who was kind enough to look after her until her last day.

"Your mom is very ill. I'm not sure she's going to make it," she said in a text message.

I'd had premonitions of my mom being very sick for several years, but I knew my mother was a stubborn woman who didn't look after herself and would keep the true state of her health a secret from everyone.

Aunt Lucy brought me up to date as to what had transpired in my mom's health for the past 18 years.

She had complications with diabetes that led to kidney failure.

She'd travelled to Mexico a month prior with a portable dialysis machine, accompanied by my brother Andrew.

The situation was peculiar because although Andrew required full-time care, he'd become my mother's primary care giver.

I hadn't had contact with my sister, Monica for more than 25 years.

If my relationship with my mother was unhealthy, my relationship with Monica was worse.

Monica had always been an emotionally volatile child, who never grew out of her outbursts, tantrums or manipulations to get her own way.

I located her via a friend of hers on social media.

We made arrangements to meet in person the next day at my mother's apartment.

Monica had a key because my mother had asked her to check on the apartment while she was away.

Seeing Monica again brought back so many unpleasant memories, but I had to be an adult about it, put my feelings aside and focus on what was important.

When I walked into the apartment my mother had been living in, I was shocked at the filth and chaos; all signs of my mom's deterioration.

I put my feelings aside.

I knew deep in my heart that my mother would not be coming home, so I suggested I stay in Canada to try to clean up my mother's home while Monica travelled to Mexico to bring Andrew and the dialysis machine back, as well as make whatever arrangements were necessary to ensure our mother had the best care possible.

She agreed on the strategy.

I booked her return ticket, and she was on a plane to Mexico City two days later.

The following three weeks were a teeter totter of emotions.

My mother's organs were shutting down.

She couldn't fight the infections that developed, one after the other.

Infections are opportunistic and my mom was an open field for attack.

She was tired and I could feel it. We'd always been connected. I could never stray far as a teen because she always found me.

I knew it was only a matter of time before the once invincible woman I called my mother would give up the fight.

She was fighting dis-ease in her body, but there were more dangerous threats nearby.

Even though I was thousands of kilometers away, I could feel entities lurking on the sidelines in her room, waiting to get at her soul.

I had visions of what they looked like, gargoyle-like demons, dark in color and low energy.

I had no confirmation or validation that what I was 'seeing' was real, but I knew that it was.

I also didn't know why they were there. I think that my mom's fears possibly attracted those beings. The only thing I was sure of was that I was going to protect my mother above all else.

Despite our difficult relationship, I loved her more than anything in this world.

Seeing those creatures was triggering. I'd been terrified of them my entire life.

Prior to that moment, I would have turned down any opportunity to fight or clear demons from any space, but I had to keep her safe.

I wasn't about to let anything or anyone get at my mother, my child in another life, so I did what came naturally to me and fought them energetically.

I had no idea if it would work, but I trusted the power of belief, the power of energy and most importantly, the power of *love*.

I put on my warrior hat, as my Great Aunt Toni had taught me, and stepped into my power.

The moment I destroyed one demon, another would appear, so I kept going non-stop throughout the day.

Prior to that moment, I'd always said that I didn't work with angels, not because I didn't believe in them, but I didn't feel I resonated with them. At least, not yet.

But for some reason, Archangel Michael had always popped up in my life, as a name, as an image and signs, so I knew he was a resource I could count on.

I called upon Archangel Michael to take over for me while I slept.

My mother needed 24-hour protection.

I 'saw' Archangel Michael fighting the demons at night, slashing their bodies in half with powerful force.

I also said the Lord's Prayer even though I'm not religious at all, but I know its power and have used it many times when trying to rid a space of unwanted entities.

Nothing else has been as effective, and again, no one ever taught me what to do in each situation. I just did what felt 'natural' to me.

Although my mother made a lot of mistakes as a mother and as a person, she did not deserve to transition into what I call 'darkness' because I do not believe in the traditional 'heaven' or 'hell.'

Her soul deserved to transition into the light and I was going to do whatever it took to facilitate that process for her.

On her last day, I sent my Aunt Lucy a message, "My mom is beginning her transition out of her body. It's almost time."

Aunt Lucy wrote back, "I agree."

I felt at peace. I'd done all I could for her.

Later that evening, Aunt Lucy called me, "Your mom passed away late this afternoon. She's now in peace."

"I felt her. Thank you for letting me know."

I sank into the sofa in my living room and gave myself permission to release all the strength I'd found within to keep myself together through the past few weeks.

A million thoughts crossed my mind, I wished things could have been different. I wished her choices had been different, and *so much* more.

But it was too late, and I had to respect the choices she made, as well as the outcomes.

Even though I'd gone through the grief of losing her several times before, nothing could have lessened the pain of the tears that flowed next.

The bond between my mother and I transcended lifetimes, roles, emotions, separations.

There was no 'surprise' happy resolution in this chapter of our story together.

Sometimes, there is no happy ending; sometimes the story just ends.

A couple of years later, I was speaking with a colleague when my mom came through.

"Gaby, your mom is here, can we talk about her?"

"Sure," I said.

"Your mom wants to say 'thank you' for what you did when she was dying."

"Oh, well she knows she's welcome." I didn't go into details because I hadn't told anyone about what I had done for my mom.

"Do you mind if I ask, how did you know to do that, because most people wouldn't know what to do."

I let her keep going. "I also don't know anyone who would have to courage to take on the entities that you fought. Gaby, they were demons!"

She *knew*.

"I didn't know. I didn't know what to do prior to doing it, nor did I know it would work. What I knew was that none of them were going to go anywhere near my mother. She deserved better."

"Wow! Well, I have to tell you that she's grateful, because what you did allowed her to transition into the light and she's now having a party!"

I smiled, "I'm glad it worked."

"Oh, it did and she loves you so much for that! She's so proud of you."

My heart was full. "I know. I felt her having a party the moment she left her body. That was my mom, the life of the party."

"Yes, she sure knows how to have a good time."

"Indeed!"

Months later, I pondered all of this again, trying to figure out the reason those entities tried to prey on my mother, but it was only through a conversation with a friend that I was able to find the answer: the reason I was shown those beings was so I would step into my Divine power.

I'd always been terrified of those entities as a child and avoided anything to do with 'evil' beings in my adult life, often refusing to accept that negative energies could even exist.

However, God knows exactly what we need and the best way to get us to step into our power.

My mom being in potential danger was just the right motivation for me. I let go of all fears and did what I needed to do, surprising myself in the process, not only at my fearless nature, but also my immediate awareness that I could achieve what I wanted to and how to do it.

Love has no boundaries.

...

I've talked about Divine intervention in other chapters, but the next chapter details yet another event that proves just how protected I've been by my guides my entire life.

Reflection Time:

Have you ever found yourself in a situation where you surprised yourself by stepping into your power and did what you had to for someone you loved without thinking about it?

How did you feel afterward?

What would it take to do that for yourself?

The Miracle of Divine Intervention

There have been many times in my life when I've known Divine intervention either saved my life or lessened the damage of potential outcomes.

At the age of 16, I was watching television in the basement of my high school boyfriend's home.

Ralph was definitely not the right guy for me and I knew it, but felt that no one else would ever be interested in me because my family was so dysfunctional.

I also felt I was the ugliest kid on the planet.

These limiting beliefs and insecurities, mostly stemming from the effects of my grandfather's abuse, led me to feel unworthy of love or acceptance.

Ralph looked like Rob Lowe. I considered myself lucky to have been chosen by him, even though I didn't know at the time that his decision to ask me out was based more on winning a bet than true interest.

I was crazy about him. I giggled every time I saw him, but he didn't feel the same about me.

He cheated on me with anything that walked, including my so-called best friends.

I stayed with him because I felt he was the only person who'd ever understand what I went through at home because his mother was schizophrenic.

His parents were divorced and he lived with his father, who was a very kind man.

We spent a lot of our free time in his dad's basement watching movies.

The basement at his dad's house was small, but large enough to fit a bench press in the middle of the floor, a small freezer and a TV against the wall.

Double sliding doors led to a bite-size backyard. We kept them closed so the basement could remain cool during the hot and humid Canadian summers.

I'm not really sure why I decided to lay on the floor beside the bench press to watch TV on that particular day, but I did.

Ralph sat on the bench press beside me.

He'd raised the back support just enough so that he could sit on an incline, and rather than placing the barbell with weights, which weighed a total of 84 Lbs., on the ground, he kept it on the press.

The two pieces of equipment were separate, and the back rest was reclinable, so he wasn't sitting underneath the barbell, but rather in front of it.

He raised his arms above his head to reach for the bar, then started spinning it with his pinky finger as we watched TV.

I could hear the bar spinning above me, but thought nothing of it. I had my hands under my head for support.

I don't know why, but I happened to look up above my head and as I did, I saw Ralph's pinky finger lift the barbell off the rest and a second later, the weight above my head fell towards me.

It happened so fast that I didn't have time to move.

I felt the weight hit the ridge of my nose and bounce.

At the same time, Ralph jumped off the bench, bent down, and pulled the weight off my face.

I was in shock.

He helped me up.

"Oh my God! I'm sorry! I'm so sorry! Are you OK?" he asked.

Confused, I looked at him in a daze. I couldn't speak.

I could see blood squirting from the ridge of my nose.

"Oh God! You're bleeding! Put pressure on your nose!" he said.

I placed my left hand on my nose to try to stop the bleeding, but it didn't work. The pressure with which the blood was coming out of my nose was comparable to that of a squirt gun.

He took me by the hand and led me into the hallway, up the stairs to the main floor of the house and into the washroom.

We didn't realize as we walked up the stairs that we were leaving a trail of blood everywhere, setting the scene for a horror flick.

I looked at my face in the mirror. My nose was swelling and turning color.

Blood continued to project onto the mirror, the walls, the counter, everywhere.

I tried putting pressure on my nose, but nothing was working to stop the bleeding.

The cut was small, but mighty.

Ralph handed me a tea towel.

Every time I took the towel off my nose, blood would squirt everywhere.

"Oh man, I think we better get you to the hospital," he said.

I looked at my nose again in the mirror. It was bigger than the last time I checked. I suspected it was broken.

"Yes, I think I need to go to the hospital," my speech was slow and cautious.

We walked down to the front door, but there was a problem. No one else was home and we didn't have a car.

"Wait here!" Ralph said.

He ran next door to see if the neighbor was home and could drive us to the hospital.

Luckily, his neighbor was home and he was a police officer.

When he heard what happened, he rushed right over.

I was already waiting by the entrance to Ralph's townhouse.

"Let me take a look at that," he took the towel off my nose.

"It was an accident," I was quick to say before I showed him.

I didn't want Ralph to get in trouble.

I showed him my nose, trying my hardest not to take my finger off the cut.

He moved my finger. Blood squirted upwards.

"Good God! OK, let me get my keys. I'll drive you to emergency."

He placed the towel back on the cut and my hand on top of it.

"Keep applying pressure," he said.

"Thank you," I said.

We waited patiently by the front door until he returned. We got into his car and he drove us to the hospital.

At the hospital, the emergency doctor examined me and put a substance on my nose to stop the bleeding.

After a few minutes, the bleeding stopped.

I was lucky I didn't need stitches.

Then he sighed, "Well, I have to say that you either have extremely strong bones, or you're one lucky girl. Had the weights hit the ridge of your nose a millimeter higher or lower, they would've crushed your face and killed you."

I looked at him with the most intense look. I went through every single detail of the event in my head in slow motion, but said nothing more than, "Thank you."

The words, "a millimeter higher or lower," kept doing summersaults in my head.

I had a strong feeling that it wasn't luck, but Divine protection that saved my life.

I had no way to explain it, it was just a feeling.

When we got back to Ralph's place, his father's car was in the driveway.

He came out of the front door as we got out of the neighbor's car.

"Oh, my God! Where have you two been? What happened?" he asked in a frantic tone.

We told him.

"Do you know what it's like to come home, find the front door open, and blood splattered all over the walls, from the basement to the kitchen and bathroom, and no one is home? I thought someone had been slaughtered!"

"Sorry, Dad," Ralph was quick to apologize.

"Sorry doesn't begin to cut it! I almost had a heart attack!"

The police officer interjected, "It happened so fast, she needed immediate medical attention, but she's OK now."

Ralph's dad was not impressed, "Come on, get inside and clean that up."

I didn't have a problem with cleaning up. Getting things sparking clean was my expertise, and part of my OCD tendencies.

Ralph drove me home later that evening.

Things hadn't been great between us for a long time.

I broke things off with him shortly after I recovered, which was just after I saw him kissing my best friend.

...

Let's continue with the theme of Divine protection. In the next chapter, I describe an event that proved to me that not only was my grandmother protecting me, but I needed to trust her guidance.

Reflection Time:

Have you ever been in a situation where things could have gone much worse but didn't?

If so, did you ever consider that it was because of Divine intervention?

If you hadn't thought of it that way, has this story made you look at that moment differently? If so, how?

The Miracle of Divine Protection

I was on my way to work early on a Sunday morning in the Spring of 2010.

The roads were practically empty at that time of the morning. I like to refer to this kind of day as "Dormingo", which is a combination of two Spanish words: "Domingo", meaning "Sunday", and "Dormir", meaning "sleep".

The two words combine to evoke the idea that Sundays are for sleeping.

Normal people sleep in on Sundays. Me, I work.

Only someone like me thinks it's a great idea to schedule herself to work on weekends from 9 a.m. to 4 p.m.

"Entrepreneurs must do whatever they need to do to succeed," was the phrase I told myself to justify my workaholic ethic.

"I have to work the hours that no one else wants to work because those are the hours that clients can get my services."

It worked for me. I was always busy.

I took the exit off an expressway in Toronto, which led northbound to my office.

The small road off the highway was deserted. Nevertheless, I drove under the speed limit, which was 60 km/hour.

I was in no rush. It had been a long time since I'd driven fast on these roads.

My type A personality was finally understanding how to 'slow the fuck down.'

Bob Marley was playing on my car's CD player. "...Don't worry...Be happy. Everything's gonna be alright..."

I'd learned that in order for me to feel less stressed, all I had to do was give myself plenty of time to get ready in the mornings, and get to work super early. That way, when the clients arrived, I'd be completely in my 'zone' and ready to serve.

Today was no different.

I saw the upcoming streetlight turn green about 200 feet away. I kept travelling at the same speed.

Suddenly, my grandmother's spirit said, "Slow down."

I have a tendency to challenge spirits when they instruct me, so I argued back, "But, it's a green light for me. Why would I slow down?"

"Just slow down," she said.

"It's Sunday morning, no one is on the roads."

"I said SLOW DOWN!" she yelled.

"OK, OK!" I said in my head and slowed the car down to about 20 KM per hour as I approached the intersection. I kept my foot on the brake and continued to reduce my speed almost to a full stop, just as I reached the intersection.

None of it made sense to me, but I was willing to surrender.

Spirits can be a pain in the rear if you don't pay attention to them.

That's when I saw an elderly man driving eastbound (on my left side) at a high speed go through the red light.

I was going so slow that I was able to observe his face in what seemed to be slow motion.

He was completely oblivious to the red light in front of him as he whizzed through.

I had no idea what else to say at that moment, except for, "Thank you."

Had I not listened to my grandmother, the old man would have T-boned me at about 80 km per hour on my side of the car. The likelihood of surviving that would have been next to none.

Tears started flowing down my face.

I was truly blessed, not just with my gifts, but with my loved ones looking after me at all times.

...

Chapter Two dealt with my first experience with energy healing. The next chapter goes into the fascinating experiences that followed...

Reflection Time:

Have you ever experienced a moment where time slowed down or sped up?

Have you experienced a hunch in a similar, unexplainable way?

If so, did you listen or ignore it? What was the outcome?

The Miracle of Self-Healing

In the year 2000, I had been dating a guy for about three years.

The story of how we met was quite funny, because I originally asked a friend to set me up with one of her friends, Paul. At the time, I didn't know his name, so I pointed to him in the cafeteria at work. However, she thought I meant his friend, Fabio.

When Fabio showed up at my door wearing a Liberace looking shirt, I didn't want to be rude and say that I actually expected his friend to show up, so I went along with it.

As it turned out, we had a great time and continued dating for three years.

However, Fabio was from a wealthy family that expected him to date someone from the same postal code, and I didn't fit the pre-requisite.

I was growing very tired of having to 'fit' into his lifestyle.

I knew deep inside that I didn't want to be married to him, but didn't know how to break the news to him.

He seemed so 'perfect,' so why end it?

However, his insecurities gave me conflicting feelings about him. He was insanely jealous, to the point where I couldn't have lunch with colleagues in the cafeteria because he'd accuse me of cheating on him, but he was a good guy at the core.

I began noticing him distancing from me, but my logical mind told me he was too methodical to cheat. I knew what he did, when, where and with whom, because we did the exact same thing every week at the exact time.

Not once did we do something different, and believe me, I tried; but every time I suggested we deviate from the routine, he'd say no.

He was the kind of guy who had to have his shirts in his closet exactly two inches apart. He even measured the distance.

My gut warned me that his jealous and controlling behavior was indicative of something deeper going on, but I refused to believe it.

I even stated that I'd put my hands on hot coals to vouch for the fact that he'd be incapable of cheating, but my gut wouldn't stop screaming, "He's lying to you! Break it off with him!"

That's when I sought the help of a psychic from Guatemala, who'd been recommended by a friend.

She dropped the bomb, "He's been cheating on you for a while with a woman who has dark hair, and tries to color her hair lighter. She wears light color lenses and is only with him for his money."

What?

Even though she'd just confirmed what my gut had been telling me all along, I still couldn't believe what I was hearing. Sure, he was insecure and extremely jealous and controlling, but a cheater?

I left feeling disconcerted, wondering if she was wrong.

Then it *hit* me.

He'd asked me to color my hair blonde, and wear blue contacts, but my response to that request was, "If you want a blonde with blue eyes, you should get yourself one."

Whenever he demanded that I wear high heels for our Saturday afternoon walks in a posh area of Toronto, my response was, "When you wear high heels for our walks, I'll wear them too."

I was also expected to wear mini-skirts so he could parade me up and down high-end shops like a trophy.

When he said that I should drive his car so I could feel what it was like to drive a luxury vehicle, I said, "My car has the same utility as your car."

Before meeting me, he'd never set foot in a Wal-Mart.

When he gave me expensive gifts and made their value known to me, I'd get angry and say, "It's not that I don't appreciate your gifts, but could you please go to a regular store instead of your usual stores to buy them?"

Every time I responded that way, he'd lose it, "Obviously you don't love me enough!"

And my response was, "I guess, I don't."

He was trying to mold me into his muse.

I knew it had to do with control, and he would never win that battle. I've always been a rebel at my core.

The day after, I caught him in the act. I just had this feeling that he was lying about where he was, so being the methodical obsessive-compulsive, and rather predictable person that he was, I went to the usual places where he took me.

Sure enough, there he was with the woman the psychic had described.

I confronted him. He acted like he hadn't been with me for a long time (typical denial) and I left.

I texted a friend to tell her what had happened.

"Are you OK?"

"Yes, I'll give you details tomorrow."

"How do you feel?"

"Relieved, actually. I've wanted to break it off with him for a long time, but didn't know how. He did me a favor."

"Relieved? Oh, no! You better get in touch with your anger!"

'A-N-G-E-R' . She'd said the unspoken word.

But what if I didn't feel anger? What if what I felt was indeed, relief? Why did I have to go into anger?

The next day, I promised my friend I'd go to the gym that evening to 'express my anger' to ensure I wasn't repressing it.

When I got to the gym, I looked around for the punching bags, then realized that even if I wanted to punch the bags, I couldn't punch them because I didn't have a set of boxing gloves and I wasn't going to hurt myself.

I opted for kicking the boxing bags, but then realized that I would likely injure my knees if I kicked them.

The only option I had left was to try to kick a bag, but hold the kick before actually hitting it.

Genius!

Unfortunately, in terms of the laws of physics and kinetic energy, that turned out to be the worst possible choice.

I've always had strong legs.

"You have the horsepower of a man in your legs!" my high school gym teacher commented after doing power testing on us.

Unbeknownst to me, every time I tried to kick the bag and held the kick, the energy had to go somewhere and hence travelled back into my leg.

I kept kicking and holding, kicking and holding, until I eventually felt a sharp pain in my inner thigh, which felt like a knife stabbing my leg.

It was so intense that it forced me to stop.

I'd had enough of 'getting in touch with my anger' anyway, so I went home to rest.

It took two weeks before the pain went away completely.

I have no idea why, but once I recovered, I got the brilliant idea of going back to the gym and do it all over again.

The second time I held my kick, I felt the pain much sooner, so I went home and decided to give up getting in touch with my anger for good.

Anger and I didn't have to meet anytime soon.

A month later, I felt a sharp pain in my inner thigh, so I called my doctor and asked if I should have an ultrasound to rule out a blood clot.

She agreed and scheduled me for an ultrasound at the hospital.

At the hospital, the doctor doing the ultrasound asked me how I got the injury because that type of injury wasn't common unless you were a professional hockey player skating at high speeds and being hit by another player, or you got hit by a car.

That was it, two options: trauma or trauma.

He asked, "Are you sure no one hit you, maybe your ex-boyfriend?"

Clearly, he hadn't met him. He would rather die than wrinkle his Liberace shirts.

I laughed, "Doctor, trust me. If I'd been hit by anyone, he'd be here, not me."

He didn't believe me, "You don't have to protect him."

"I'm not."

He diagnosed me with a calcified hematoma and added 'myositis ossificans' to it as the cherry on the cake.

Myositis ossificans is a condition where your muscles pretty much turn to stone because the brain mistakes muscle tissue for bone and mistakenly sends calcium to repair the soft tissue.

I prefer to call it the 'Medusa syndrome', except, instead of turning others into stone, I was turning myself into stone. This was a reminder that A-N-G-E-R and I weren't such good friends.

I knew he'd jumped to the wrong conclusion.

He referred me to a surgeon to have the hematoma looked at. "He's one of the best in Toronto," he said and I was seen immediately.

The plastic surgeon examined me and scheduled me for exploratory surgery right away out of fear that it may be cancer.

What?

The nurse told him it would take three weeks to get me in.

"We don't have three weeks," he said.

Gulp. Not something you ever want a doctor to say in front of you.

I was scheduled for ambulatory surgery three days later.

On the day of the surgery, he walked into the surgery room and said, "This is ambulatory surgery, so you're going to be in and out. OK?"

"OK."

"Let's see what we've got here."

Instead of looking at my ultrasound images and report, he asked, "Where does it hurt?"

I was laying down face up on the table and hesitated before I pointed to the inner thigh in my right leg, wondering if this was standard procedure. It just seemed too casual.

"OK! I'm going to inject you with a local anesthetic."

"You're not going to look at my ultrasound?" I asked, hoping he'd say, "Of course, silly! I'm a surgeon, not a butcher!" But he didn't.

He scrubbed his hands, dried them and put on his surgical gloves.

Then he grabbed the syringe and inserted it into a vial of what I assumed to be the local anesthetic and proceeded to inject me in a couple of places on my inner thigh.

He waited a few minutes and pressed against my leg with his finger.

"How does that feel?"

"OK, I guess. I can feel it, if that's what you mean."

"No, you can't. It should be numb by now."

"OK, if you say so."

He grabbed a scalpel and asked again, "Where does it hurt again?"

I hesitated to answer, "You're joking, right?"

"No."

I was still hoping he'd say, "Psych! Just kidding!" But he did not.

I lifted my head and pointed to the exact spot where I felt the pain one more time.

"OK, you can lay down and relax now."

Relax? How could I? Was this a bad dream?

I felt the scalpel cutting into my skin.

I kept trying to lift my head to look at what he was doing. I didn't trust him. Each time, he told me to keep my head down.

"Mmm…should I be telling you if I feel what you're doing?"

"You shouldn't be feeling anything."

"Well, I do."

"No, you don't."

What's with this guy?

"Yes, I do."

He tested the validity of my claim by poking me in a few spots with the scalpel and asking, "Do you feel that?"

I felt like I was in a Verizon commercial.

After a few pokes, he yelled out, "Holy crap! You can feel it!"

"Yes. I can. I have the same problem when I go to the dentist. They have to give me more anesthetic than the average human. My dentist says it's the dose she'd give to a horse."

He proceeded to inject me with more anesthetic.

"I just injected you with enough anesthetic for a horse!"

No shit Batman!

I couldn't feel a thing after that and kept my head on the table, hoping, praying for the best.

After a few minutes, he said, "I don't understand!"

That's another thing you ever want to hear your surgeon say in the middle of surgery.

"What?" I asked.

"It's not there!"

Another thing you never want to hear your surgeon say in the middle of surgery.

"What do you mean, it's not there?" I asked.

"I mean it's not there! The hematoma isn't there! I've gone all the way down to the bone and I can't find it!"

I couldn't help myself, "I'm no expert, but don't you not think it would've been a good idea to look at my ultrasound images before cutting me open? You know, just saying…"

No answer.

He put the scalpel down and yelled, "Nurse!"

I was pretty sure things weren't going to get better.

A blonde woman poked her head in the office. "Yes?"

"Get me her ultrasound images please!"

She looked perplexed, but brought them to him anyway, "They were here all along. Didn't you see them before?"

I interjected, "Nope, he didn't."

She looked at him, shocked, but trying to play it down.

He gave me a dirty look, gave her the file back and sat down beside me again without saying a word.

I had a strong feeling that he said nothing because he'd just screwed up in a major way.

He closed me up and used surgical tape to secure the dressing over the stitches.

"Nurse!"

The nurse popped her head back in. "Yes?"

"Schedule her for an MRI right away!"

She left and came back a moment later, "The earliest they have is three weeks from now."

"We don't have three weeks!"

Another thing you don't want to hear a surgeon say in front of you.

She left and came back a few moments later, "She's in for next week."

"OK."

I couldn't help myself again, "Don't you think the MRI should've been done before the surgery?"

No answer. Dirty look.

It took me six more months before I found a doctor to diagnose me properly, and that was thanks to a friend who worked in the insurance industry, who referred me to a trauma specialist at one of Canada's top rehabilitation facilities in Toronto.

The trauma specialist, a woman of Eastern European decent, and her resident looked at my diagnostics and reports.

Her extensive experience came across without question.

I told her about my ordeal from the very beginning, and for the first time in a long time, she gave me solid answers.

"First of all, it is absolutely possible to have this kind of injury even if you're not hit by a car. The problem is that you didn't get it looked at right away, so it's too late now to do something about it. Had you seen a doctor immediately, we could have prevented the hematoma from calcifying. Be glad that the plastic surgeon didn't find the hematoma, because if he had removed it, it would have started the whole process all over again and you would've had more tissue damage. So, his mistake was actually a blessing in disguise. It's going to take another 18 months for the hematoma to come to full maturation, which means it will turn into bone. Once that happens, we'll do the ultrasound again and remove it only if it bothers you or causes too much of a restriction on your range of motion. Otherwise, you can just live with it."

I went home feeling much better and decided to apply the skills my Great Aunt Toni had taught me all those years ago.

Every day for eighteen months, I applied energy to my leg with the intention to dissolve the calcified hematoma.

Eighteen months later, I had the follow-up ultrasound and went to the trauma specialist to get the results.

She looked confused when she read the report and looked at the image.

Then she turned to me, "Did you have surgery to remove the hematoma?"

"No, why?"

"I don't understand."

Oh, oh!

"What do you mean?"

"It's not there anymore."

I smiled, "That's a good thing, no?"

"Well, yes, but bone doesn't just dissolve."

I smiled again.

"What did you do?" she asked.

"Energy healing."

"What?"

I explained how I placed my hand over my inner thigh and set the intention to dissolve the hematoma.

She was visibly confused, "Well, whatever it was, it must've re-absorbed back into your body."

"Yes. It must've."

...

The next story details how our spirit guides are always there at the right time and place.

Reflection Time:
Have you ever experienced the power of energetic healing?
If you have, what was your perception of it and outcome?
If not, and after reading this story, would you be open to it?

The Miracle of Spirit's Love

Just a week after I got back from my magical trip to Costa Rica, I was on a plane on route to San Jose, California to join over three thousand women at a soulful business women's conference.

I kept my promise to myself and to my mother after she passed, to live life to the fullest and not worry about how I was going to pay for things.

This trip to Silicon Valley was another item off my bucket list.

The conference got underway with presentations from women leaders, who shared their experience in a traditionally male-dominated business world.

The conference leader taught us about the advantages of incorporating a female, soft energy into our business models vs. trying to fit the traditional model of masculine energy in business.

We participated in phenomenal exercises that connected us with our spirituality, breaking down preconceived belief systems about money and business.

Many breakthroughs happened over the weekend, but the most important one for me was during a sitting mediation.

I saw the same white angel I saw in Costa Rica come down and hover above my body again. She penetrated my abdominal area with her hand. My mind went into…*OK, now I'm starting to worry. What do I have? Is it that serious?*

I said to myself, "Whatever this is, keep it coming God. I love seeing this angel."

I was grateful for the experience and trusted that God had my back.

Through the weekend, I also felt my mother's presence with me at all times, especially during an 'angel whispers' exercise where we wrote down three things that we wished our parents had said to us as children.

I wrote down, "I'll never abandon you. I love you. I have your back."

We then took turns whispering those things to the person in front of us.

The words flowed out of our mouths, evoking tears in a back-and-forth sway of unconditional love.

My turn came to be a receiver.

The stranger in front of me whispered, "You are loved. I'll always be here for you. You are not alone."

At that moment, I felt my mom's spirit brush the side of my face with the most caring and loving energy.

I surrendered to the overwhelm of emotional outpour triggered by such a magical experience.

There was no doubt in my mind, body or soul that my mother was with me, letting me know how much she loved me. Even though she never actually said the words, "I love you," to me when she was alive, she was finding ways to convey her love for me in spirit.

The tears never stopped flowing throughout the hour-long exercise.

The miraculous aspect of that exercise was that everyone heard exactly what they were needed to hear. 'Source' energy makes no mistakes.

The emotional releases were cathartic.

Then came an exercise to bring up the reasons why so many of us held back from promoting or growing our businesses.

I looked down at the workbook in front of me, read the question and waited for the answer.

Suddenly, I began to cry.

"What's wrong?" asked one of the women in my group.

"I just realized why I've hesitated promoting my business."

"Oh, boy. Why?"

"I'm afraid to die, and I'm terrified of being seen!"

"What?"

"The last time I had a business, I worked myself to the ground. I almost died and I don't want to do that to myself again. Also, when I was a kid, being seen by my grandfather would lead to a beating. I now realize that my entire corporate career, I made myself invisible because unconsciously, I didn't want to be seen. It's all tied to my childhood trauma!"

"Wow, that's powerful!"

"Yes, but I also realize that this time, I have the knowledge and the tools to do it differently. I don't have to work myself to the ground. I can be seen. I am safe."

I returned home with a new sense of freedom to work on my business by setting parameters that were conducive to a healthy and balanced lifestyle, putting myself first and having the business work for me, not the other way around.

I decided to adopt the mantra of, "I work smarter, not harder".

It didn't happen overnight, but I let go of the fear that there wouldn't be enough if I gave myself a day off, which turned into two days, and now less with the right tools, so I don't have to sacrifice income streams.

…

My mom made many mistakes as a mother, but after her passing, she proved to me she'd always be there for me, as you'll see in the next chapter.

Reflection Time:

Take a sheet of paper and write down all the things you wish your parents had said to you as a kid. Then I invite you to say them to yourself and feel how wonderful it feels to hear them coming from you.

The Miracle of a Mother's Love

No one is all good or all bad, not even religious leaders.

Although my mom made a lot of mistakes as a mother and in life overall, she was the strongest, most positive and persevering person I've ever known.

She loved sports, even after being permanently injured in a car accident, which affected her ability to participate in them. But she still loved adventure, camping and exploring new places.

Everything I am today is because of my mother.

Whereas some people like my stepmother lived plagued by fear, my mom lived life fearlessly.

She left Mexico for Canada at the age of 33, as a single mother of three children, two of whom were special needs, not knowing the local language or having any guarantees that she would make it financially.

All she knew was that she wanted to give my siblings a better chance in life.

She was my superhero, despite our differences.

My mom was also intuitive and could astral travel, but never told anyone about it until she overheard me speaking with Toni.

"Oh, please, I astral travelled as a kid all the time! I've been to China, other planets…it's no big deal!"

"Oh, but it is! If only I'd known, if you'd only said something, I wouldn't have felt so different from everyone else around me!"

"You're always making such a big deal of things!" And just like that, she dismissed my need to know, share and understand different abilities.

After she passed away, I decided to visit a friend a couple hours away from Toronto and was travelling on highway 401.

Traffic was heavy; stop and go, slow and fast, stop and go.

There were moments when I was able to travel at the speed limit, but was still cautious of the traffic ahead. I'd had near misses in the past in that type of traffic because the clear traffic portions can be deceiving.

I was travelling under the speed limit when I realized that traffic had come to a stop again, so I slowed down, but had a really bad feeling in my stomach that I wasn't going to have enough room to come to a complete stop.

As I got closer to the stopped car in front of me, I realized I was right.

I pressed the brake pedal as deep as I could, but knew I was going to make impact. There was no other way to go either. There were cars on either side of me.

I braced the wheel and prepared myself for the inevitable.

All of a sudden, I felt my mom's energy around me and in front of me. It happened fast, but it was almost as if she slowed down time.

I felt her energy move to the front of my car and stop it just before I hit the car in front. I felt the force like a bang, but without the noise.

I blinked as my head jolted forward a bit. For a moment, I thought I'd made contact with the car.

At the same time, the front of my car took a dive, and then settled back down.

I opened my eyes. The silver SUV in front of me was centimeters, if not millimeters, away.

I knew there was no way I wouldn't have hit that car had my mom not intervened.

I felt a sense of simultaneous shock and release. I couldn't contain the tears.

My mom had just saved my life.

At that moment, I remembered all the times I'd asked her to protect me, not to leave me alone with her father, my brother, or others when I didn't feel safe.

She always said I was overdramatizing and dismissed my pleas for protection, and each time, I was hurt by the people I had feared would hurt me.

Then she'd dismiss the fact that they'd hurt me.

However, in spirit form, she was able to be there for me and jump in with fierce strength and power to protect me.

I felt light in my body as I took my foot off the break and moved ahead with traffic, trusting I was safe.

Thank you, mom. I love you.

...

Mothers are amazing, but so are fathers. My dad, like everyone else, had good and bad qualities, but what I loved about him the most were the gifts that he passed onto me…And yes, you better believe he takes credit for them.

Reflection Time:

Have you ever witnessed the power of a mother's love in a supernatural way?

If so, how did it affect your perspective from that moment forward?

If not, do you think you'll be more conscious of the innate power that each of us holds within?

The Miracle of a Fallen Hero

My dad was my first mentor, but unlike Toni, Lalo wasn't a teacher. He just talked about his interests in the occult and his experiences reading palms.

He led a bit of a double life. Working in finance didn't give him much freedom to talk about paranormal activity with anyone other than close family.

He'd also raised my three half-brothers as atheists, so I'm not sure that he was as open about his gifts with them as he was with me.

However, my Stepmother Bruna was aware of his abilities and trusted them, for the most part. My father told her the moment she was pregnant and the exact day that she would give birth to each of my brothers.

While I was on my holidays visiting my father, my brother, Roberto and his wife at the time, Camila, came over to my dad's house for a visit. They were going through a rough patch in their marriage, but my brother hadn't said a word to anyone.

I sat across from Camila and him in the living room. My father was sitting on a sofa chair to one side, and my stepmother sat beside me.

As we caught up on everything going on in our lives, I noticed a black cloud hovering over Camila's head.

I knew it couldn't be good. I sensed that they were having issues, but didn't want to tune into what was happening out of respect for my brother's privacy.

The last time I'd had a vision around him, I saw his ex-girlfriend cheating on him while on a business trip to Spain.

When she returned from her trip, she broke up with my brother, which came as a shock to everyone in the family, especially my brother.

However, I had a strong feeling it had to do with my vision.

Only months later did the truth about her infidelity emerge.

I didn't care much for Camila, but respected his choice.

She was a hypochondriac and eccentric in her ways, but I didn't care as long as he was happy.

After about an hour, I couldn't handle her energy any longer, so I excused myself.

"I'm so sorry, but I need to go upstairs and take a nap," I said.

"But, it's five in the afternoon," Roberto said.

"I have jet lag."

"There's only an hour difference."

"I know, but it's been a long day, sorry."

"OK," he said with doubt.

I went upstairs and watched TV until they left a couple of hours later.

I heard my dad walk up the stairs and go to his room.

I knew his routine well. He was methodical. He'd change into his pajamas, go to the kitchen to grab some milk and cookies, then go back upstairs to watch TV until about 9 p.m., and then fall asleep.

At 8 p.m., I went downstairs in search of a snack.

My stepmother was sitting at the kitchen table smoking a cigarette. She always said she'd rather die than stop smoking. She'd been smoking two packs of cigarettes per day for over 40 years.

"Did they leave?" I asked in a low voice.

"Yes. Why did you leave so early?"

I hesitated, searching for just the right words. I didn't want to be insulting, "I just couldn't be around her energy anymore. She had a black cloud over her head. I don't know what's up with her, but she's either depressed or sick, or something."

"Really?"

"Oh, yes! Her energy is repulsive."

"Wow, OK."

The next morning, I invited my father and stepmother to breakfast at a local restaurant.

Sunday morning breakfast at that particular restaurant was a family tradition until my dad got too sick.

We sat at our usual table and asked for café con leche.

As we waited for our coffee, my dad blurted out, "I don't know what's wrong with Camila, but she had a dark cloud over her head yesterday! Something's not right with her."

My stepmother, who was about to take a sip of her coffee, put her cup down on the table and laughed.

"You saw it too?" I asked in shock.

"Yes! Why? Did you?" my dad asked.

"Yes!"

My stepmother looked at both of us and said, "Like father, like daughter!"

"What do you mean?" my father probed.

"Well, you both see the same things and pick up the same energy about people."

"Well, it is hereditary. Roberto has the same gift, even if he's in complete denial. He's super intuitive," I said.

"Ah yes, but he'll never admit to it. He doesn't want anyone to look at him the way they look at us," my dad said. He was right. My brother would never let anyone know how gifted he was.

Years later, after my father was diagnosed with a chronic kidney disease and reached the end-stage, he had to make a tough decision: accept a kidney transplant or die.

He always said he'd lived long enough and didn't want any of his children to donate a kidney to him. He wanted us to have both our kidneys just in case one failed.

Thankfully, his nephrologist said, "That's very honorable, but let's put you on the transplant list just in case."

My dad was in his seventies, but because he was so methodical and disciplined with his diet and following instructions from his medical team, he was allowed to be on the transplant list.

In the meantime, he received hemodialysis treatments to keep him alive. At first, he received a couple of treatments a month, but eventually he required several treatments per week.

End-stage kidney failure is disheartening. There's a point where not even a machine that cleans your blood is effective in keeping you alive.

There's also an increased chance of blood clots, so you need to be given blood thinners to prevent them, which complicates matters.

My dad experienced two blood clots while on hemodialysis, one in the brain and one in the lungs, but he made it through both.

Towards the end, his brain cognitive function decreased, hand tremors set in, and slow, painful deterioration began to happen throughout his body.

Just as we were giving up hope that my dad would get a new kidney, the phone rang at 1 a.m. one night.

It was my dad's nephrologist, Dr. Marquez.

My stepmother answered the phone. She and my dad's relationship had deteriorated to such a point that she was incredibly hostile towards him.

They'd been sleeping in separate rooms for years and their interactions were rarely amicable.

I truly believe she wanted him dead.

I could hear the conversation through the walls in my room. "My husband told you before Dr. Marquez, that he doesn't want a kidney," she said.

I was shocked when I heard her, but luckily for my dad, Dr. Marquez pressed on, "Can you please put your husband on the line?"

"Fine, but he's just going to tell you the same thing."

She woke my father up and handed him the phone. I got up and stood at my dad's door, hoping he'd say yes.

My dad was startled at first, but paid close attention to Dr. Marquez say, "We have a kidney. Can you be here in an hour?"

My dad was almost in tears. "I'll be there as soon as I can."

He jumped out of bed faster than I'd ever seen, got dressed, and then my stepmother drove him to the hospital.

I waited at home and prayed that all would go well.

At the hospital, his doctors ran a few tests to determine if my dad was a match for the kidney.

Unfortunately for the donor's parents, their 21-year-old son had been murdered during a robbery.

My dad was number four on the transplant recipient list, but quickly moved up to number one when it was determined that he was the only person compatible with the young man's kidney.

He was rushed into surgery. By the next morning, he had a new lease on life.

He was kept in the ICU for a few hours after the surgery to ensure he didn't reject his new kidney.

Once the anesthetic wore off, my dad became aware of his surroundings.

Dr. Marquez came in to check on him. My dad was doing remarkably well. So well, that he was taken to a private room the next morning.

My dad described what happened next: "I woke up that morning still groggy from the anesthetic, but felt good; better than I'd felt in years! The nurses came in to check on me several times that day, and everything was going well. That evening, I had a visitor, which surprised me because they weren't letting anyone in to see me just yet. It was a young man, whom I now know was Raul, the boy that died, whose kidney I have inside of me."

"He did?" I asked in bewilderment.

"Yes."

"That's amazing!"

"He sat down on my bed and we talked. He told me his last name and described everything that happened, as well as his aspirations in life. He wasn't resentful about his murder because he was able to help people live on with his organs."

"Wow!" I wanted to hear more.

Then he described how Dr. Marquez went into his room the next day to check on him.

My dad was curious and asked, "Dr. Marquez, would it be possible to meet Raul's parents to thank them for my kidney?"

Dr. Marquez stopped looking at my dad's chart and said, "How…why…who told you the donor's name?"

"He did," my dad said.

"What do you mean, he did? He's dead. He couldn't have given you his name."

"Oh, I know that, but he came to visit me last night. Well, his spirit did, and he told me how he died, his last name, all of it. We had a great conversation for about an hour."

"Look, I'm not sure who gave you his information, but you must know that donor names are completely confidential. I need to know who gave you that information!"

My dad repeated himself.

Dr. Marquez shook his head, not really knowing what to make of it, then headed for the nursing station. My dad could overhear his conversation with the nursing staff.

"Who released the donor's name to the patient in 308?"

The nurses responded in unison, "No one, Dr. Marquez."

"Well, he knows the name and that's strictly confidential information!"

"We didn't release the information Dr. Marquez," the head nurse reassured him.

"Then who did?"

"We have no idea. No one else has gone into his room except for nursing staff," she said, and then added, "Did he say who told him?"

"He says the boy's spirit came to visit him last night."

Silence.

The next day, my dad felt well enough to take a walk down the hallway. As he passed the nursing station, he saw a woman walking towards him.

As she passed him, he noticed that she was holding a small gift box in her hands.

My father knew intuitively that it was Raul's mother.

My dad made his walking round. Upon his return, one of the nurses called him over to the nursing station and handed him the gift box saying, "This is a gift from the donor's mother."

My dad smiled, "Please tell her I said, 'thank you' if you see her again, or if you can call her on my behalf."

She smiled.

My dad went to his room with the box on hand.

He placed it carefully on a table beside his bed. It was a box of chocolates with a note that read, "We're glad our son was able to save your life. God bless you. Enjoy."

My dad smiled from ear to ear.

When my father passed away in 2021, I felt his spirit leave his body and zoom around like Peter Pan. He was ecstatic after leaving his body.

I was upset over his passing and said, "Look, Dad, I know you're happy you left your body, but keep in mind I'm human and mourning you, so could you take your elation down a few notches till I have time to process?"

"But this is so cool!" he said, like a curious child.

"Yes, I know Dad, just let me cry a bit, will you?"

"OK."

Then he showed me a panda from the movie, "Kung-Fu Panda," in relation to my brother Roberto.

I sent Roberto a message, "Why is dad showing me Kung Fu Panda with regards to you?"

"Oh my God! That's my favorite movie!" Roberto said.

"Did Dad know that?"

"No, but he does now!"

We both had a great laugh over it.

After that, he came through during a Reiki treatment, but he showed up with an entourage of Ascended Masters, including Jesus.

I was somewhat surprised, but not really. My dad was a warrior in his own way and very well connected politically in Mexico, so it didn't surprise me that he'd walk in with la crème de la crème of spirit guides.

He began directing me in the treatment and I, of course, argued back.

"Really Dad? All of a sudden, you're the expert in energy healing? Really? I suppose now you're going to tell me that I'm gifted because of you?"

"Yes."

"Whatever dad! Of course you would!" I laughed, but was grateful for the intervention.

...

The next chapter looks at the special abilities that I've mentioned in this book in a more descriptive way, so that you may understand and potentially identify your own superpowers.

Reflection Time:

Have you ever felt the soul of a loved one as they were leaving their body?

If so, how does it make you feel to know that there is no such thing as 'death'?

Has reading this story altered your perspective about what happens after we die?

The Miracle of Your Superpowers

People often ask me if I learned to be a psychic or if I was born this way.

As the stories I've been sharing show, I may not always have understood what my abilities were, but they've always been a part of me. This has been my 'normal' from the time I was born.

However, I'm going to let you in on a little secret: everyone has these gifts, but not everyone is aware of them, or knows what to call them. Some people dismiss them, and others block them.

I'm an empath, which basically means I can feel other people's, animals' and plants' pain, emotions, and suffering.

Yes, event plants feel and suffer. Plants have consciousness, and studies have proven that they're able to communicate with each other. They also react positively or negatively to energetic stimuli, like music, sound and words, the same way as water.

Until I learned how to control this ability, it was not fun at all. I go into detail about this in the clairgustation section.

Empaths also feel energy from people, things, places, animals and plants.

Then there are the other **superpowers** or **'gifts'** or **'clairs'.** 'Clair' is a French term for 'seeing' used to refer to various types of extra-sensory perception using all five senses. I had no idea that these abilities had labels until my Reiki Masters sent out a newsletter on them and I started researching them, but I have most and they're strong.

I've heard some people refer to their 'gifts' as 'curses' because they don't want to see, hear, feel or perceive so much from their environment.

I can understand that feeling, but when you learn to manage the intensity of these abilities, as well as when to allow them to be 'on' and how to turn them off, they become great tools for navigating through our human experience.

The abilities are closely related to our senses. I like to use the metaphor of being a big walking antenna tower that senses energy.

Everything about us is part of the antenna network: our energy, thoughts, blood, cells, DNA, bones, fluids, skin, hair, eyes, ears, tongue, organs and nose.

I want to also emphasize why it's so important to be properly hydrated if you want to be healthy and develop your intuition.

Water is a conductor and we need it to function effectively on all levels, so I invite you to stop your excuses about why you don't drink enough water and hydrate, unless it's a contraindication for you.

I won't talk about all of my abilities in this book, just the most relevant.

Please keep in mind that many overlap, so don't get caught up in technicalities.

Claircognizance

Claircognizance basically means that I know information without having prior exposure to it.

This gift is very annoying to people who know me because they want to know where I get my information and I cannot explain it.

I just know things with conviction. It's like having access to a massive energetic library that encompasses the entire universe, and the information is delivered to me instantly.

A great example of this is when I knew that many employees were going to be fired by my former employer without having prior access to the information.

My colleagues assumed I had insider information, but I didn't. I just knew.

I also know when mass media is spreading misinformation, which is most of the time, unless you're watching or listening to independent sources.

This is the reason why my Great Aunt Toni told me not to watch TV or listen to radio.

Another example is when a former boss asked me to be her partner and I said, "No."

I had no idea why, but knew it wouldn't be a good idea. It wasn't personal, I just knew to turn down the opportunity, no matter how good it seemed.

Clairaudience

Clairaudience is also known as the ability to communicate with souls, God/Source energy, my Higher Self, Mother Earth and spirit guides, including extra-terrestrial beings.

Clairaudience is the gift that is commonly referred to as mediumship or channeling.

When I do mediumship readings and energy healing sessions, I'm communicating with spirit guides (mine or the client's), who show me what needs most attention in the client's life at that moment, especially if it is a physical symptom, and how to assist their healing.

I tell clients that the message they'll receive is what they need to hear vs. what they may want to hear, and hopefully the two match.

I used to question the messages and would have discussions with spirits in my head before relaying the messages to the client, until I learned that my job is simply to relay the message and get out of the way. It isn't for me to understand the message, just pass it on.

However, now and then I do challenge them, but only to get clarity for my clients.

Channeling *and mediumship* are often used interchangeably.

There is a type of channeling that is a bit more complex, and that is when a reader allows spirits to enter their body and use it as a vessel to communicate with the physical world. Some call this jumping (when the spirit doesn't ask for permission and takes over the body) or walk-ins (similar, but there is a contract agreed upon).

I don't agree with doing this, as it's too invasive, but I have experienced short moments where spirits have used me to experience a physical experience through me, if just for a very brief moment and only part of my body (arm).

The way this manifested was by me making the same mannerisms as the spirit and speaking in the same tone as they did, which is another way of validating their presence to their loved ones. When this happens it's quite comical, yet effective.

Also, when communicating with souls, I ask them for validation that will make sense only to their loved one(s).

The validation can be in the way of songs, words, phrases, images of situations, pictures, jewelry or other personal belongings, places, food, habits, behaviors, emotions, symptoms or symbols.

Each 'symbol' is different and unique.

The communication can be very much like a game of charades, where I have to figure out through the senses what the image is and communicate it as best as possible.

Sometimes I get glimpses of color, but most of the time the images are shaded like film or photography negative slides or reels.

This is why it can be a bit of a challenge to make out what I'm being shown and if I can't make it, I set it aside and ask for another symbol, until something makes sense to the client.

I also have to be discerning as to how I convey the information because the receiver isn't always ready to receive it.

I try as much as possible not to filter information, but sometimes spirits use words or terms that are inappropriate and I have to soften the words or choose an alternative way of delivering the information without being so direct.

This of course, as long as I'm not taking away from the 'voice' of the spirit.

An example is a soul that used a lot of foul language in life. If I tried to say things without the swear words, it wouldn't be as authentic.

When this happens, I apologize ahead of time and deliver the message.

Clients usually laugh when I do this because it validates their loved ones right away.

Spirits keep their personalities after they pass, so if they were dirty-minded in life, for example, they'll have no filters after they pass, and it can be quite embarrassing.

Also, spirits don't always know how to communicate effectively, or their loved ones may not remember the given symbols as clearly or as easily as intended by the spirit. A colleague and I joke that we have to 'teach spirits how to be dead' by guiding the communication process.

As mentioned above, m*ediumship* is often interchanged with channeling.

I want to bring up a controversial subject. Some mediums believe that we cannot communicate with the spirit of a departed person unless they've been dead for at least six months because this time period is required for the soul to do a life review, and hence they will be busy doing the review.

I was never trained by others to communicate with spirits and therefore, do not have any limiting beliefs when it comes to my ability to communicate with souls.

Time doesn't exist in the quantum field. It has been my experience that I can communicate with souls as they are leaving their body, right after they die, and at any time after they pass.

But this does not mean that communication is guaranteed. Sometimes spirits have nothing to say, it may not be the right time for the receiver, or I may not be the person who is meant to deliver the message.

This is why I teach my students that nothing is cast in stone. Everyone is right. The approaches may be different, but in essence everyone is correct. Your beliefs define your reality.

Your truth is your truth, so go with it and if anyone tells you that things must be one way or else…thank them for the information, but seek your own truth.

The ability to communicate with spirits and other beings is probably the gift I'm most grateful for because in the process of communication with them, I'm able to feel the love that spirits have for their loved ones, and you cannot put a price on that.

As an empath, it can be overwhelming, but beautiful.

I learned to protect myself with crystals, grounding, an energy bubble, bringing my aura in, and other protection and energy hygiene techniques to make sure that I'm a clean channel for my clients and that my energy is protected from absorbing anything that doesn't belong to me.

Clairolfaction

Clairolfaction is the ability to sense a scent from a spirit as a sign to validate their presence to you, such as the smell of perfume, flowers, sweat, smoke, coffee, wood or food.

When all else fails, spirits will resort to whatever they think will be most effective to get you to acknowledge their presence.

Also, if Grandma used to love wearing Chanel No. 5 perfume and people knew it as her signature scent, she'll bring that up right away and I can get a sense of it.

However, if Grandma knows that I don't like perfumes or wouldn't recognize it, she'll use another symbol that would be easier for me as the interpreter of the message.

It's all about making communication easier.

Clairgustance

Clairgustation or Clairgustance is the ability to get a taste in your mouth as a sign to validate a spirit's presence, as well as pick up information from the food you taste, which is a lot of fun.

For example, if the spirit smoked, they may give you a taste of an ashtray in your mouth, or if they had a thing for a particular dessert, they'll give you that in your mouth, as long as you can recognize it.

Years ago, I was speaking to a chef who asked me to try a sample of a dessert he'd made for a client.

I was a bit surprised by his request because he was very protective of his cooking and I'd never had a chance to taste his food before, but people come to me for the truth.

We met at a coffee shop.

He pulled out a sample of his specialty and placed it on the table in front of me.

The whole thing was humorous because it seemed very secretive. I felt like a food energy sommelier.

I moved the dessert towards me, carefully taking the wrapper off and examining it closely.

I took one bite and closed my eyes, taking my time to savor it and identify some of the ingredients in it.

He waited.

I could sense his nervousness.

I had no idea why the idea of me tasting his food brought him such uneasiness. After all, he was an accomplished and experienced chef.

After a moment, which I'm sure seemed like an eternity to him, I delivered my review, "You've done better."

He lifted both of his eyebrows.

"You rushed through this. You wanted to get it over with and move on to the next thing."

"You can sense that from one bite?"

"Yes. You didn't put any passion or love into it. Am I right?"

"Yes. I was tired and just threw things together. I didn't feel like making it at all, but had to deliver the order this morning."

"Well, I'm sure your client won't notice, but you definitely do much better when you put your heart into your cooking."

"Wow. How do you do that?"

"I've no idea. I just do."

He never asked me to taste a sample of his food again.

This particular 'gift' became so intense for me, that there was a point when I had to stop eating meat because I could sense the suffering that the animal I was eating had gone through when it was killed.

I'd see flashes of how they had died and felt their suffering.

The pain and suffering were so overwhelming to me, that I couldn't place any animal protein in my mouth.

Subsequently, I became vegan and was vegan for about two years.

But that didn't solve anything. I also started becoming aware of the pain that plants had gone through when cut or yanked from the ground and prepared for consumption.

Yes, plants and trees are sentient beings too, and I felt all of their suffering.

I became aware of the communication between their root systems before I read about it and learned about in *Music of The Plants* .

Then I thought, "Now what on earth will I eat?"

Jack, my intuitive mentor suggested sunlight, but I'm a foodie, so no.

It was ridiculous, so I had a conversation with Source that went something like this: "OK, Universe. I understand that my gifts are getting stronger and that the lesson behind this particular gift was to become aware of the sacrifice of other beings for my sustenance. However, if this keeps up, I won't be able to live unless you can make it possible for me to survive simply with the energy from the sun, and although I know that's possible too, I really do enjoy eating. Let's face it. I'm a foodie! So, why don't we do this, I'll give thanks for every sacrifice that had to happen for my nourishment and I stop sensing so much from the food I eat? Can we agree on that?"

And just like that, the 'gift' of clairgustance decreased to an acceptable level.

Clairsentience

Clairsentience is the ability to read information from objects, spaces and people (if you touch their hand, for example).

The art of psychometry, which is the ability to read information from objects as you hold them in your hand falls under this category.

I can sense the energy of a room, city, space, item or body, and I can touch (or not) a piece of clothing or furniture, even walls, and get information from them.

I can also write a person's name on a piece of paper, place my finger over their first name and do a reading on them that way, though I don't have to do it at all in order to read them.

All I have to do is focus on their energy from the person who wants me to read them.

I became aware of this gift after taking a course of controlled remote viewing (CRV), just out of curiosity and then realized that I could perceive the energy in written words this way.

If you think about it, clairgustance could also fall into this because you're touching the food with your tongue and reading information from it.

Some psychics will tell you that they need to have the first and last name of the client, date of birth, and/or other details in order to read the person, but I don't.

I do, however, like to write the person's first name on a piece of paper and run my finger over it just for fun. It's amazing how much information I can pick up from it.

Everything that we perceive as solid, liquid, gas or otherwise, has the capability to store information in it. The same way that a computer is able to store information in it.

Every event, thought, emotion, and physical object or matter is made up of energy, and I read energy.

Energy is stored in the Field and we are part of the Field. Everyone has access to that information, as long as they're open to it and are able to avoid the distractions of the three-dimensional realm.

I guess you could say I'm the monitor and speaker that connects to the computer and projects or communicates the information contained in it.

Another analogy is that I'm the cell phone tower that passes the information from the waves that go from cell phone to cell phone. The client and another person or soul are the cell phones.

What I find amusing is that people have no issues believing that a cell phone can work, but doubt that readers can read information from people in very similar ways.

Everything is energy, and energy can be sensed and read by receptors.

Astral Projection

Astral projection is the ability to project your energetic body (soul) from your physical body and go into the ethereal plane, where you can visit other people, places, or events.

The majority of us astral travel during our sleep.

I wanted to learn how to astral travel consciously, so I read *The Astral Projection Guidebook* by Erin Pavlina.

It was a great resource because she didn't just teach you how to do it properly, but how to protect yourself, your body, and what to do in case of encountering negative entities in the ether.

I had to do several attempts because the tingling sensation in my body as my energetic body left my physical body was overwhelming and too uncomfortable.

Finally, after a few attempts I became more comfortable with the discomfort and I reached the ether, but just as she'd described, I got excited and came back to my body immediately.

I attempted astral travelling again after my mom's passing.

I felt blocked from the anger I felt towards my mother and figured that if I left my body, we could have more of a face-to-face conversation, but the moment I started separating from my body, I felt my mom's energetic hand pressing on my chest to push me back into my body.

"Not now," she said.

I didn't question it. I knew my mom was protecting me.

I'd been too angry and emotionally distraught dealing with the mess she'd left behind.

Strong negative emotions lower the strength in our energetic body, which opens opportunities for negative energies to penetrate the energetic field.

This is why we have to be consistent with our energetic hygiene and the protection of our energy field.

I had to wait, mourn, process and regain my emotional balance before attempting it again.

However, I wouldn't recommend astral travelling or developing intuitive gifts to everyone.

There are people who already have a hard time deciphering between reality and non-reality, and I do believe that further expanding their gifts could be counter-productive to them.

Telephathy

Telepathy is the ability to communicate with others (humans and souls), through thoughts, as well as read their thoughts.

I was able to do this with my father and mother as a teen.

Anytime I wanted my father to call me, I'd focus on him and set the intention for him to call me, and he would call saying, "I got this thought in my head that I had to call you."

My mother could find me anytime, anywhere. I could not hide. She'd just tune into my energy, drive to the place, and found me.

She even knew when I'd travelled to another country when we were estranged.

My husband laughs when I finish his sentences for him, or when I say exactly what he is about to say. "It's like you're reading my mind! You may as well just have the entire conversation by yourself."

Pre-cognition or Clairvoyance

Pre-cognition or clairvoyance is the ability to 'see' the future before it happens. This is one of my oldest 'gifts', or rather, one of the first I became aware of.

One of my earliest memories of visions was around the age of seven, when I was counting the money in my piggy bank.

I was proud I'd saved most of the money I got for my allowance from both my father and grandmother.

I sat down on my bed, emptied my piggy bank and counted the coins, reveling at the wealth I'd accumulated.

Then I put all the money back in and carried the vault, carefully hanging on tight so it wouldn't accidentally fall and break.

Suddenly, a vision flashed in front of me in slow motion. I saw the piggy bank slip off my arms, fall to the ground and break into thousands of pieces. Coins flew everywhere.

I was so upset by the vision, that I held onto it even tighter as I made my way into the den, where I kept my loot.

As I crossed over the threshold, I tripped over my feet and watched the vision become a reality faster than it had in my vision.

I stood looking down at the broken pieces in disbelief, full of mixed emotions, including anger, sadness and disappointment.

Many more visions would follow.

Years later, when we were living in Canada, I was about fourteen when I had a dream that my grandfather had been hit by a car and his leg was broken.

When the weekend came, I made my weekly call to Grandma Minnie and asked how my grandfather was.

"Oh, he's OK now dear, but he was hit by a car earlier this week. A woman was driving, didn't see him as he was crossing the street and hit him. He suffered a broken leg, but thankfully that's all. In fact, he was so 'OK' that he was flirting with the lady and her friend."

I felt guilty because at the time, I thought my dreams were the cause of the events vs. premonitions of the future.

At fifteen, I was about to get into my mom's friend's car, a Thunderbird.

My mother was upstairs, so her gentleman friend, Rick was going to give me, Ralph (my boyfriend at the time, the one in the story in Chapter 18-The Miracle of Divine Intervention), and his best friend John, a ride to the mall.

John was short with a strong build, just a year older than me, but not the smartest kid.

He was sitting on the trunk of the car, waiting for me to get into the car, when I had a vision of him getting his pant leg caught in the wheel of the car. He was pulled underneath the car and run over.

I saw every detail in slow motion, as a holographic movie in front of me.

"Please get off the car!" I yelled.

"Why?"

"Just get off the car!"

"No. Come on, get in. I'll ride on the trunk till the end of the driveway."

"Get off the car!"

"No!" He tapped the hood to let Rick know that he could start the car and move slowly.

I refused to get into the car until John got off the trunk.

Rick, not realizing that John was in any danger, put the car in gear and drove very slowly towards the end of the driveway.

Within seconds, John was dragged under the car, just as I'd seen in my vision.

I yelled as loud as I could, "Stop the car!"

Rick stopped as soon as he felt the car go over something.

He got out and walked quickly to see what had happened.

John was laughing.

He got up, brushed himself off and said, "That was fucking cool!"

"That wasn't funny at all! You just got run over by a car! Are you OK? Did anything break?"

"I'm fine!"

John wasn't the brightest lightbulb, but he must have been the strongest because all he had were scratches and a ripped pant leg.

...

I knew every time I applied for a job, that I had the job before I went for the interview.

I passed it off as confidence, but deep down inside, I knew.

I just knew that all I had to do was show up and the job was mine.

During my corporate days, my boss and mentor, Nathan, who was aware of my 'gifts,' often asked me to give him my take on individuals and/or situations.

One day, he walked into my office and said, "I have two guys coming in to see me today at 3 p.m. I want you to go to my office at 3:15 p.m., say 'hi,' and leave."

"OK."

I did just as he asked.

Later that afternoon, he popped into my office again and asked, "So?"

"They're both snakes pretending to want to work together, but they can't stand each other. They're in it for themselves and are full of ego. Within six months, they're going to walk into your office to say, "Either he goes or I go."

"You think so? They seem like they really want to work together."

"I know so."

Six months later, he walked into my office and said, "How the fuck do you do that? They just walked into my office and said, "Either he goes, or I go."

I laughed.

When the company we worked for was put up for sale, I watched who came in and out of the offices, paying close attention to their energy.

I knew the type of organizations they worked for and why the were there, just by observing them and 'reading' them.

I told all my colleagues that the company would be dismantled and reduced in size from thousands of employees to a small fraction of that.

No one believed me and chose instead to believe the lies the executive team was feeding them.

Two years later, there were only 1300 employees left, out of many thousands.

My colleagues claimed that I must have had 'insider information', which I did, just not the type they were thinking of.

Psychokinesis or Telekinesis

Psychokinesis or telekinesis , is the ability to manipulate matter with energy.

If you ever watched the movie, "Carrie," or the movie or TV show, "Iron Fist," you'll witness examples of telekinesis.

I had to learn this skill and if I hadn't learned it, I'm not sure I'd be where I am today.

It was after I did my Reiki level 1 & 2 training that I became more curious about having physical proof that the energy I was using on clients was affecting them on a physical level, not just energetic.

It's not as if I didn't get great feedback from clients that it worked, but I wanted more concrete evidence. I'm skeptical by nature, so I prefer to get proof of things, even with my abilities.

One of my clients suffered from contractures in her right ankle as a result of MS.

Unbeknownst to her, I would build an energy bubble around her right ankle before concluding her Reiki treatments, to prevent her ankle from contracting.

I never told her I did this. I just did it and hoped for the best.

One evening, I had just completed her treatment, but was tired and decided not to do the bubble.

After all, according to me, she had no idea I did that, so I figured she wouldn't miss it.

"OK, we're done for today. Please take your time getting up."

"Ah, you forgot something Gaby."

"I did?"

"Yes, my bubble."

I was stunned, "You know about that?"

"Oh yes. Please don't forget my bubble. I feel it every time I get a treatment and as I'm walking home, and the entire time between treatments. It really helps prevent the contractures on my ankle, so please do it."

The next day, I called my Reiki Masters and I told them what had happened.

"I know this is amazing feedback, but I still want physical proof that what I'm doing is affecting people's physical body," I said.

"OK, so come to our spoon bending class," Ethan said.

"Spoon bending class?"

"Yes. Sign up for it and you'll get your proof."

I didn't think twice about it and signed up for the three-hour class.

I brought my friend, Randy, with me because I wanted him to understand my world a little better.

He was also an IT guy and I knew he needed to get out of his head a bit more.

At the start of the class, Ethan and his wife, Lyn, asked us to take the spoons in front of us and try to bend them.

No one could.

"OK, now put your spoons aside and let's begin," Ethan instructed us.

We were led through two hours of guided meditations, then videos from various movie scenes from Star Wars and The Matrix, which showed examples of telekinesis.

In my head though, I thought, "Yeah, but that's Hollywood."

Then I reminded myself of Toni's teachings, "Remember there is no such thing as solid objects. We are all space."

The bells in my head started going off.

Once again, I was remembering information that I had been privy to so many years ago.

At the two-hour mark, my type-A personality tendencies started to get antsy.

I raised my hand. "I don't mean to be rude, but it's a three-hour class and we've been meditating for two hours. I'm just wondering when do we get to bend spoons?"

"That's why you've meditated for two hours, so you can get out of your head and bend spoons."

"Oh."

Dah!

"Get your spoons out."

They walked us through the process, one step at a time.

"Now, bend your spoon!" Ethan said.

I followed the instructions carefully and pressed both ends of the spoon towards the center very gently until the spoon bent like an accordion.

My friend Randy, who was sitting beside me, was in disbelief.

He tried to bend his spoon, but was unable to.

"Remember, there is no spoon, Randy."

As soon as he tuned into the truth, he too, bent his spoon.

He was in awe. "If you hadn't brought me here, I never would have believed this was possible."

From that day forward, he read almost every book he could get his hands on about metaphysics and watched documentaries about ancient discoveries.

I'd turned him into a believer and created a bit of a monster, but in a good way.

Shortly after that, he confessed to me that he could see spirits all his life, but only when he's angry.

However, he'd never told anyone because he was terrified of being rejected by his family, who were devout Catholics.

Today, I carry a bent spoon in my purse. I have another in my office and at home, which serve as a constant reminder of the power we have within.

A few months later, I was walking my seven-month-old puppy on a beach in Toronto, accompanied by a male acquaintance.

We came across a rare site: an aggressive Golden Retriever.

When we walked by, the dog was off-leash and it charged at kids, other people walking on the beach, dogs, and anything that moved.

The male owner actually seemed to enjoy watching other people's fear as they hurried along to get as far away from his dog as possible.

He was about as self-centered as it gets, and continued smoking his cigarette as he observed his dog run after people.

Seeing this happen, I picked up my puppy and carried him against my chest as we walked past the aggressive dog.

At that moment, the owner decided to hold on to the dog by its collar, as the dog barked and growled.

We walked past them as fast as we could.

When we were approximately fifty feet away, I turned around to see if it was safe to put my puppy down again.

That's when I saw the owner let go of the dog's collar, as if giving the dog permission to charge towards us.

I was tired of the dog's and owner's attitude by then, so I handed my dog over to my acquaintance. "Here. Whatever you do, don't put him down on the ground."

"OK," and he walked backwards, watching me.

I turned around and started walking towards the dog, which was still running towards me. Its eyes were focused on mine and mine on his.

I've no idea how I knew to do this, or how I got the courage to do it without fear of being seen by everyone around us, but I physically gathered all the energy around me with my hands, got down on one knee, visualized the energy becoming a sphere of white light, which I projected towards the dog with force.

It was as if something had taken over me. I had no idea what to expect when I did it, but somehow, I knew it would work to stop the dog from attacking.

The dog stopped suddenly about 20 feet away from me, let out a loud yelp, turned around with its tail between its legs and crawled back to its owner.

The owner watched all of this unfold, and when he saw his dog crawling back in fear, he yelled, "What the hell did you do to my dog?"

I stood up, looked straight at the guy, turned around and walked away.

The dog's owner didn't have to know my intent was never to hurt his dog, but rather to show him that its behavior was unacceptable.

Just because his owner was an asshole, it didn't mean the dog had to be punished for it.

Then I asked my male acquaintance to hand me my puppy back.

"What on earth just happened?" he asked.

"I have no idea, but it worked. Hopefully, he'll never be aggressive again. Let's go before I get taken away by The Black Hats (a.k.a. clandestine government operatives)."

"The Black Hats?"

"Never mind. Let's just go."

Energy Medicine

Energy medicine is the ability to channel universal energy through your body onto someone else's body, whether in person or remotely, even by proxy, in order to facilitate healing.

When you balance a person's energetic field, the body heals itself.

Dis-ease appears in the energetic body before it gets into the denser layers, and into the physical body.

By treating the energetic body from stress and negative energy, we can prevent dis-ease from presenting in the physical body.

I believe that this is a 'gift' and learned skill for me.

Although I never needed to learn how to do energy medicine and basically heal people by just sharing the same space as them, I do believe that learning about The Silva Method, Qi Gong, sound healing and Reiki, along with my empathic abilities, helped me identify and hone in on my abilities, as well as develop the gift of **Medical Intuition.**

Also, as I've grown in my spiritual development, I've become aware that I'm now capable of switching into higher levels of consciousness (dimensions), which is where I do healing sessions from.

A man who visited my booth at a show observed me for some time, but I was busy with readings, so I didn't have time to speak with him.

He approached one of my nearby colleagues wanting to know more about me because he said that he's always had the ability to see auras. In fact, when he walks around on a daily basis, that's all he sees, auras.

He wanted to know more about me because he'd never seen anything so beautiful in his life. He said, "When she connects, she connects straight to Source and works from higher dimensions. She glows unlike anything else I've ever seen! There was also a silvery white liquid-like light going from her heart onto the client." Another friend, who can also see energy, made the same observation.

My colleague couldn't answer his questions, but she was kind enough to let me know what he'd said to her.

I thanked her because it validated what I always say to clients, "We're never disconnected from Source. It's our awareness that changes, but never the connection."

There are thousands of energy medicine techniques from all around the globe. It is my belief that they all work, at different levels, but the most important aspect in the healing process is intention and it is even more effective when in trance state. This is why I promote meditation as much as I do. When we meditate, we allow our body to heal naturally.

Medical Intuition

Medical Intuition is the ability to tap into people's energetic aura and identify current symptoms they may be experiencing, past symptoms or injuries they went through, or future ailments they may experience if they don't change their lifestyle and/or habits.

I've tapped into fractures, gunshot wounds, trauma and many other conditions. Not fun, but they validate the information I perceive to clients.

When I say I tap into their symptoms, I actually feel them in my body, regardless of when they occurred.

During the process, I'm guided to the part of the body or organ that needs attention. Sometimes spirits point to the organ and sometimes they draw it out of the body holographically so I can identify it.

Then I get a sense of what their symptoms have been and feel those in my body. I can feel dizziness, the urgency to urinate, extreme pain, electrical or dull pain, headaches, fogginess in the brain, inflammation, nausea, and some symptoms are quite bizarre, but when I tune into them, clients are shocked.

Sometimes what can happen when I'm reading a person, is that I tap the energy of people close to them instead of their own. Sometimes they're family, friends or co-workers.

When this happens, the reading tends to be directed at those individuals because they need help more than the client.

This is why energetic cleansing is so important. Our energetic fields are constantly entangled with other people's fields, and the entanglement can affect us in positive or negative ways. Healthcare workers and people who work in funeral homes can be the most complex to read for obvious reasons.

I do not diagnose when doing medical intuition readings. I prefer that people go to a doctor to get the necessary diagnostic tests and a proper diagnosis.

However, people often come to me after becoming frustrated with the medical field because they've been unable to give them answers or they intuitively know there's more to their symptoms than has been discovered.

Through medical intuition, I'm able to direct them to the right practitioner to get better answers, be it a naturopath, homeopath, or another alternative medicine practitioner to help them get a proper diagnosis or find complimentary treatments for their conditions.

I've had several people come to be asking how long they have left to live, and my response is always the same, "Wrong question to ask."

Then I get a look of confusion and I clarify, "The question you should be asking is, how should I live my life from now until the end, because neither you nor I have any guarantees."

Then we dive into their passions and take the focus away from dying and shift it to living.

I also explain to them that I've seen many people in stage 5 cancer go into full remission, simply through the power of belief. Nothing is written in stone. Our mission is to live life to the fullest, instead of coasting through life because coasting never serves anyone.

Passion is what drives us, and if they don't know or they forgot what they're passionate about, I remind them.

They often leave with a smile on their face and a new sense of purpose.

Automatic Writing/Drawing

Automatic writing/drawing is the ability to receive information from spirits/Source/your higher self through writing and/or painting.

This is an awesome and fun ability.

You ask a question, put your pen to paper and wait for the answers to come.

As they do, you write them down without questioning if it is real or if you're making it up.

All you have to do to get an answer from Source is ask.

In hypnosis, we know that the unconscious mind has no other option but to come up with at least one answer when you ask a question. That's its job, to problem solve.

This is why I promote delving into your creative outlets as much as possible, because they truly open up the communication channels with the Divine.

I always say that what I write doesn't come from me, but Source.

The moment I sit down to write, the information just flows. It's a meditative process during which I often go into trance and it becomes so intense, that I can spend easily twelve hours per day writing without stopping. I have to force myself to eat and even go to the washroom because I can forget to do so.

Automatic writing is a tool that some mediums, like Tyler Henry, use to receive or facilitate or channel communication with spirits.

Seeing and Reading Auras

Seeing and reading auras is the ability to 'see' the energetic field of things, plants, people and animals with the naked eye.

An aura reader can also receive information from the aura without seeing the aura, but feeling it instead, which is what I do.

The aura can be stagnant or moving, and when it's moving, it can move slowly or fast.

It also has density, and from my experience, the denser the aura, the more the person has gone through in life in terms of difficulty or trauma.

When I read a person's aura, I penetrate the aura layer by layer and I am given access to different information as I go through the layers.

The information or type of information is never the same for anyone, though I tend to perceive medical symptoms first.

Sometimes I perceive past life information. I always say that what I tune into is what will make the most impact for the client at that moment in their life.

Every reader will tune into different information, depending on their own outlook, perspective, personality, and belief systems, as well as how they resonate with the client.

You can get three different readings from different readers because each will tune into different aspects of your field.

Readers also filter information as we tune into it.

Some readers have the ability to see the aura as a clear haze, while others can see a white, blue or greyish outline, and some can see the full range of colors in the auric field.

The colors mean different things, as does the intensity and clarity of the color. The aura colors usually coincide with the colors of the chakras or energetic centers of the body.

I actually prefer to close my eyes and read the aura to eliminate any distractions or judgements my conscious mind may make about the person I'm reading.

Clearing Energy Fields and Helping Spirits Cross Over

Clearing energy fields and helping spirits cross over is the ability to cleanse the energy in a room, animal, plant, person or item, such as crystals, or transmute the energy from a lower vibrational energy to a higher vibrational energy.

Helping spirits cross over means facilitating their detachment to the physical realm and transition fully into the spirit realm.

This doesn't mean that once they cross over they cannot communicate with us or won't be 'present' and guiding us, but it means they've let go of their attachment to a physical item, space or person.

This 'clearing' can be achieved with a variety of tools, such as smudging, sound healing, mantras, prayer, water, placing them in the sun, or under the light of the moon.

However, it's important to understand that these are just tools and it's the intention that makes it happen, not so much the tool.

I love buying antiques and used goods because of my belief in the 3 Rs (reduce, reuse, recycle).

However, I recommend cleansing anything you buy used and even new, because the items are often handled by many people before they get to the end user.

Each interaction can leave an energetic imprint on the item, and if those people haven't practiced energetic hygiene, you may pick up their energy debris, or emotional energy unconsciously.

A few years back, I bought a table I needed for doing live shows.

When I got to the apartment building where I was to pick up the table and saw the guy bring it down, I immediately sensed that there was a spirit attached to it. I knew I'd have to clean it before using it.

The spirit was that of a young man who'd died by suicide. He was angry in life and angry in spirit because he was still attached to the material realm. Once spirits transition fully, the only emotion they experience is *love*.

Even though I've said that once spirits cross over all the issues they had in life become 'clear' to them and they release them, when they attach to the physical realm, they can also attach to those emotions that no longer serve them.

I got home and cleaned the table physically, as well as energetically, with sage. However, it didn't work to get him to leave, so I said, "Look, I'm not about to battle with you to get you to leave, so I'm going to tell you how this is going to go. You need to walk towards the light. Everything you ever yearned for in life, all the love, compassion and understanding that you wanted, is in the light and you know where it is. Your loved ones are waiting for you there, as well as your guides. You basically have two choices: the first is that you stay here and be smothered with love every moment of your attachment, or cross over and live in love energy. Either way, it's going to be love, so pick one."

The spirit chose to cross over and his negative energy was gone instantly.

Are all crossovers that easy? No.

A few years ago, I was asked to do a treatment at a large and well-known business.

The moment I grabbed the handle of the front door, I had visions of a particular group of organized crime, as well as a person who'd been murdered on the property.

I hesitated before going into the building, took a deep breath and thought to myself, *Oh boy...this is going to be interesting!*

I walked in, introduced myself to the receptionist and asked to be directed to the room where I was to do the treatment.

I met the client, did the treatment, and left.

As soon as I got to my car, I called the person who referred me and asked her not to refer me there again because of what I 'saw.'

She was blown away by my comment because she knew it was true.

"The owners want to know if you can help clear the negative energy in that place because it's affecting their business."

"Oh, man…"

"Pretty please?"

"Fine."

The owners arranged for me to go after hours during the summer, so there was still natural light coming in through the windows.

The staff member who met me at the door gave me the key to lock up afterwards, and left me to do my thing on my own in a 20,000 sq. ft. facility.

I took a deep breath and locked the door behind me.

Clearings are unpredictable. As a medium, I never know what I'm going to encounter, which is why putting a price to a clearing isn't always easy. Some are simple and some are extremely complicated.

I walked around the entire building to get a feel for the space. It wasn't pleasant. There was more than one spirit present, some more positive than others, but there was definitely unfinished business. I could sense a darker energy.

No one thought to tell me where the main light switch was, so when I walked around, I purposely searched for the main power switch in preparation for sundown.

Many of the rooms were locked, so I had no idea if I would be able to find it.

There were also multiple entrances to the building, so it was like a hunting expedition.

Frustrated after almost half an hour, I made a few calls and finally someone tried to explain where I could find the location of the main switch.

I ended up in a mechanical room in the center of the space. But by the time I found it, there was no natural light coming in. I was in a room where I couldn't see my hand in front of me.

I used my cell phone as a flashlight.

However, the person giving me instructions didn't quite know which light switch among the 30 or so switches was the right one.

I could feel the spirits in the room with me, which didn't scare me, but it wasn't an ideal situation for me.

I told the person on the phone, "Look, I'll come back another day because trying to find the right switch in pitch darkness is next to impossible. When I come back, please tell your staff to leave all lights on, and show me how to switch them off when I'm done."

I went back a few days later, burned sage around the perimeter, and did another walk through of the place.

My senses were fully present with every step. When I got to the center of the main room, I had a vision of someone being shot in that spot and felt a sharp pain in the biceps muscle of my left arm.

The pain was a deep burning pain, unlike anything I'd ever felt before.

I knew at that moment that the pain was from a gunshot wound, although I'd never been shot before.

As a medical intuitive, I feel the symptoms that clients or spirits experience in the present or past. With experience, I've learned to connect just enough to feel them, but disconnect immediately, so I don't go through the trauma myself.

I held onto my left arm as I felt how the victim had bled out from the gunshot. I had to massage the pain out and once the pain had dissipated, I continued walking through the space.

I directed each spirit to cross over as I walked.

After a couple of hours, I decided this job was bigger than I'd anticipated and would require help.

I left and asked my friend Octavio, another medium from Mexico, who was living in Toronto at the time, if he'd help me.

Octavio can see spirits and does energy cleansings through Mother Gaia, but he's not an empath.

I'm an empath, but don't see spirits as easily as he does. However, I can feel them and there's an advantage to that. They cannot hide from me, but they can hide from people who can only see them and not sense them.

I thought our combined approach would be much more effective than me working solo.

We met at the location a few weeks later.

Octavio walked in, looked around and said, "I don't see anything."

"They're hiding," I said.

"What do you mean, they're hiding?"

"They know you can see them, so they're hiding. They can't hide from me. I'll feel them no matter how much they try to hide. Keep walking. Go to the back rooms."

"Interesting," he said as he continued walking.

I followed behind him about eight feet away and lost sight of him as he went around a corner into a closed off area.

Suddenly, I heard him say, "Oh my God, Gaby! You were right! They were hiding!"

"How many are there?"

"Hundreds!"

"I knew this wasn't a one-person job."

"This place was built over a cemetery, but there's also a portal here. That's why there's so many spirits. We have to send them back through the portal and close it."

"OK, and I take it you know how to do that?"

"Yes."

"Phew! Let's do this! What do you want me to do?"

Octavio told me exactly what to do and when.

I watched him as he worked to get the spirits into the portal. All the while, I could feel the energy in the room form a vortex, which was so strong, I had to hold onto the wall behind me for support.

Suddenly, I heard the sound of weights dropping on the ground, "What the hell is that?" I asked.

"They're trying to distract us! Stay focused!" he said.

"OK!" I yelled.

It felt like we were in the midst of a tornado inside the building, which lasted for about a half hour.

I was dizzy and felt nauseous no matter how much I held onto the wall.

Finally, he said, "I won't be able to get them all in. I need to close the portal now!"

"Do it!"

Moments later, the energy around us stopped swirling.

I felt a tremendous amount of relief. My body relaxed a bit.

"That was awesome!" Octavio claimed in victory.

"Was it?" I said sarcastically.

"What a rush! We need to start a ghostbuster company!" he said with pride.

I could feel the excitement in his heart.

"No." I was quick to respond.

"Why not? Don't you think it'd be cool to do this for people?"

"Dude, if you think I'm going to go through what we just went through for what they paid for this service, you're out of your mind."

"I hope you charged at least $500. This is worth at least that!"

"Not even close. It was a favor and I'll give you all the money they offered to pay me, but there's no way in hell that I want to do this again. No way, no can do, nah ah!"

"Come on! We work well together!"

"I know we do, but you're right, this was a lot of work. But no one, unless they do what we do, will appreciate what we just went through in order to clean this space. That was a job worth several thousand dollars, and we just cleared run-of-the-mill spirits, not even demons. Unless they were willing to pay for it, I would not do it. They have no clue what we potentially expose ourselves to; the dangers, the skills required to identify what's truly going on or how to get rid of whatever is in there, so NO."

"So, you'll think about it?" he said laughing.

I drove him home and made a call to arrange to meet with the owners the next day to hand back the keys.

I told the owners of our findings, but that we didn't clear all the spirits.

If they wanted that done, we'd have to back at least one more time or more, but it wouldn't be for free. I gave them a much higher number than they ever imagined.

They gave me $100 and I transferred it to Octavio right away.

"That's it?"

"I told you it was more of a favor and that was for the two times I went there."

"Do they want us to go back?"

"They didn't say, but I don't expect to hear back from them after I told them how much it would cost. Like I said, unless they were there and were able to experience it from our perspective, with all our senses, they are oblivious to the danger, skills or work involved. As far as I'm concerned, we're done."

Octavio was grateful for the money, and I didn't bring up the subject again.

Today, I show clients what to do on their own clearings and encourage them to step into their power.

Next, we're going to explore the way that my knowing of God's existence has shaped my opinions about organized religion.

Reflection Time:

Let's get real. Do you think you may have ignored your gifts prior to reading this story?

How many of the above abilities do you believe you may have, regardless of how strong each may be?

Would you be more willing now to honor your abilities? If yes, how?

If not, what holds you back?

The Miracle of 'Conviction'

I had just turned twelve when my grandmother insisted that my siblings and I to do our First Communion.

She insisted because she knew that my parents would likely refuse to do it in an effort to get back at each other.

We were also about to move to Canada with my mother, so it was now or never.

I wasn't keen on doing it, but went along with it just to make her happy.

Grandma Minnie arranged for me to meet with the priest who would conduct the ceremony, so I could 'confess' my sins for the first time.

"What would you like to confess, my child?"

"Nothing," I said with certainty.

"That cannot be true, you must have something to confess."

"No, I don't. I don't lie, or steal, or anything else that would require me to confess."

"I don't believe that, my child."

Patience has never been one of my strengths and I was getting really tired of his condescending tone. "I'm telling the truth."

"No, you are not."

I had no idea how to convince this caricature that I had nothing to confess, but I knew I wanted to get this battle over with, because I likely didn't stand a chance.

I figured I'd kill two birds with one stone, so I said, "I lied today."

Bad to the bone!

"See? I told you."

You sure did.

My grandma's eyes sparkled as she watched the three of us walking towards the priest to take our first 'Body of Christ.'

No one else attended the ceremony.

I was just glad to get her off my case about not being able to participate in communion.

Little did she know that I did not plan to set foot in a church again.

I found sermons utterly boring and the whole idea of confession was hypocritical from my viewpoint.

The idea of a punishing God was also a made-up interpretation by someone other than God.

God has spoken to me from a very young age.

I knew the 'rules' taught by the Church were man-made.

Nothing was cast in stone, not even the Ten Commandments.

When I said, "God is inside of me," as a child, I meant it. I believed it and always had, without having been exposed to that information from humans.

God made me aware of it at a young age and I wasn't about to question direct messages from God, but I questioned most messages from humans.

The patriarchal nature of the Church made me feel uncomfortable.

I saw no reason as to why women were not allowed to lead, or why nuns had to 'serve' priests, why certain information was 'protected' by the Church and disseminated on a 'need to know' basis, or completely kept from the people.

None of it made sense to me.

When my uncle Juan asked me to be his maid of honor at his wedding in Mexico, I refused because I'd be required to confess, and I had rejected the idea of confession long ago.

The other reason I refused was because I thought his marriage was a complete façade.

He was not a faithful man.

I asked him, "Are you sure you want to do this? You're the last person in the world who should do this. No judgement, but it's like pretending to be a cat when you're a dog. It's not in your grain to be married or with only one woman. Please, just be the best dog you can be and stop pretending to want to be a cat."

"Please do this for us. It would make me so happy if you did," he said.

"Fine, I'll go see the priest, but I'm warning you, I will not lie just to make him happy."

"OK."

I walked 20 minutes from my grandmother's house to the Catholic Church in our neighborhood, wearing running shoes, jeans and a t-shirt.

Making a good impression was the last thing on my mind.

My uncle set up the appointment for me, so the priest was expecting me.

I walked into his office through the side of the church.

The office was filled with books, a large desk and a couple of chairs for visitors.

He was sitting on his chair and pointed to one of the guest chairs, silently guiding me to have a seat.

"I understand you're here to confess because your uncle wants you to be his maid of honor."

"Yes."

"Well, let's begin then."

"OK, so since it's a confession under the eyes of God, I suppose I'm allowed to say anything, correct?"

"Yes, of course."

"Alright, let's start with the fact that I don't believe in the Catholic Church, especially because of the massive abuse of children by priests and nuns throughout history."

The priest raised one eyebrow.

"Furthermore, the patriarchal nature of the church is outdated, repressive, archaic and oppressive."

He raised the other eyebrow.

"Third, the Bible has been changed so many times throughout history, that it seems more like a great piece of literature than religious history, with the purpose to manipulate the actions of the audience who reads it."

He raised both eyebrows.

"The idea that God is a punishing entity is a lie. And while we're at it, I don't believe that churches should be asking people for 10% of their wages, so that the Vatican can enjoy such wealth and opulence."

He didn't raise his eyebrows. I could sense he was becoming more and more rigid.

"When it comes to confession, what's your take on a twelve-year-old being forced to lie in order to satisfy the requirement of confession?"

The priest shifted his body on his chair, trying to hold back his simultaneous expression of surprise and offense before asking, "What do you mean by that?"

"I mean that when I had to do my First Communion at that age, and told the priest I had nothing to confess because I was indeed a really good kid, he told me I was lying. So, in order to satisfy the requirement of confession, I made up a lie in order to be believed."

"I see."

I could tell he was holding back what had likely now turned into anger.

"Well, from what you've told me, I can tell you that being a member of the Catholic faith requires commitment and dedication. It is clear from your comments that you're not a member of the Church, nor are you committed to following our teachings or abiding by our community rules, so I don't see how you could serve as maid of honor at your uncle's wedding tomorrow. It's best that you don't."

"That's what I thought. Thank you for your time."

I got up and I walked back to my grandmother's house with a smile on my face that screamed, *Relief*!

When I arrived, my uncle asked with anticipation, "Well?"

I repeated verbatim what I'd told the priest, expecting my uncle to be disappointed in me.

"Well, technically, you confessed."

"Right?"

"Yes."

"That's what I thought."

The next day, I got dressed, attended the service at the church, got in line for communion and when I reached the same priest that I'd 'confessed' to the day before, I looked him straight in the eye, extended my hands in front and continued looking at him as he placed the host in my left hand.

I grabbed it ever so gently and placed it in my mouth as slowly as I could, without taking my focus from his eyes.

I smiled and said, "Thank you."

Then, I turned around and walked back to my pew, passing my father on the way, who whispered in my ear, "You have balls. Not even I would have been so defiant."

I smiled as I sat down.

...

Reiki or other energy healing practices are only some of the ways that people can balance their energy. The next story describes my personal experience using a machine that blew my mind when it came to identifying issues within my body.

Reflection Time:

What are your thoughts on the religious beliefs you grew up with, if any?

Have they changed over time? If so, how?

Would you be less afraid now to develop your own belief systems?

Do you understand now that you're meant to discover your own beliefs and that it's OK for them to change as you grow?

The Miracle of Energy Healing Technology

Shortly after learning Reiki, I came across a Biofeedback machine at a clinic where I worked.

There was a woman there who used the machine on clients, and I'd heard wonderful feedback from them about this unique machine.

One gentleman in particular raved about the fact that the machine saved his life.

He'd had a scan done and the scan showed that he may be dealing with inflammation potentially caused by malignant cells; however, because biofeedback practitioners, like all other alternative medicine practitioners, cannot diagnose, the biofeedback practitioner referred him for further testing and diagnosis by his family doctor.

The client had just undergone his yearly physical and everything came up 'normal', so when he went back to his doctor asking for a second look, the doctor dismissed his fears and asked him to stop listening to 'quackery'.

"Just humor me, please," he insisted.

"Fine, but you'll see that it shows nothing. These people are lying to you and robbing you blind!"

A couple of weeks later, the tests results came back positive for prostate cancer.

His doctor was in shock, but refused to admit that the biofeedback machine had any merits.

Thankfully, because the cancer was detected at such an early stage, the man was able to get treated immediately without any invasive treatments or negative side-effects.

Years later, I came across a biofeedback machine again while in Mexico City at a health and wellness show.

The woman demonstrating the machine offered me a demo, which I was quick to accept.

She secured the rubber bands around my ankles, wrists and head, careful ensuring that there was rubber to skin contact.

Then she turned towards the machine and started reading the information that the biofeedback machine was picking up about me.

"You have a subluxation on vertebrae T3-T5."

I opened my eyes wide in surprise. "Yes," I said with hesitation.

"You have a history of…" and she went through a list of pretty much every ailment and injury I'd experienced in my life.

I couldn't believe what I was hearing.

"Wait, how does the machine know so much about me? I feel like I'm seeing the best psychic ever!"

"It tunes into your energetic body." She kept going, "You also have abandonment issues with your mother and father."

Gulp.

The sales woman smiled, "Has anyone ever told you the color of your aura and how wide it is?"

"Yes, a friend who sees auras told me my aura is green, which means it's very healing and it's at least six feet wide, which makes sense because I practice Reiki."

She smiled, "Is that what you think?"

"Yes. Why else would it be?"

"Let me ask you something, do your friends ever tell you that they love being around you, and that they feel so good after spending time with you?"

"Yes, of course! I attribute that to my charming personality," I said with a wink.

She laughed.

"It isn't?"

"No."

"Then why do they love being around me?"

"Because you heal them. Anyone who shares the same space as you is automatically healing their body. I hate to disappoint you, but it has nothing to do with your personality."

"So, I never had to learn energy medicine to facilitate other people's healing? People heal by just being near me?"

"Yes, that's how powerful you are."

"So, you mean to tell me that I wasted my money taking Reiki?"

"Pretty much," she said laughing.

"So, what you're saying is that I should get some T-shirts that say, "Hang out with me, I'll heal you?"

She laughed again, "Yes."

"Wow."

"Indeed. You're very, very special."

The memories of my finger healing, surviving 84 lbs. of weights hitting my face, the calcified hematoma disappearing, and so many other moments rushed in.

It wasn't a coincidence, or luck. I was a walking healing machine. *I just happened to walk into walls and trip over myself a lot.*

I went home and began to read as much as I could about energy medicine, scalar energy machines and techniques, as well as the science behind energy medicine.

At first, it was overwhelming because there are thousands of techniques and my creative mind wanted to learn them all and buy every machine out there, but my spirt guides said, "You don't need to. Trust yourself."

"Not even the Biofeedback machine, which I really, really want to buy?"

"No. You do the same without the machine."

"Frustrating!"

"Why? You should be glad you don't have to spend that money. You can identify issues and facilitate healing without it. Why do you want a machine?"

"Because it's a tangible."

"Ah…you still don't need it."

"Fine." I pouted like a little kid who didn't get her toy.

After learning about various techniques and machines, I came to the realization that regardless of the technique or equipment, they all work, but the most important aspect of energy medicine is intention.

The machines may add consistency, but intention is everything in healing, manifestation, intuition, all of it.

Then comes believing in your own power, having the courage to step into that power, and trusting that you are capable of making all of it possible.

Then you must trust, and by that, I mean blind trust. There are no tangibles in energy work.

This is where most people get stuck, because they look for solid evidence, and nothing is 'solid' in the quantum field.

Energy isn't tangible in the way we expect, but when you trust in your own power, magic happens. Magic is the tangible.

Everything is energy, and because energy is easily malleable, working with it is easier than we've been led to believe.

Years later, I did a reading for a woman who sold biofeedback machines. She was shocked at how much I picked up about her and her health from reading her aura.

I told her about the fact that I've wanted to get an energy scanning and healing machine for years, but my guides tell me I don't need one.

She laughed, "They're right! You don't need any machines!"

Although this type of equipment exists and works to balance our energetic field, I've talked about other situations where people have also used energy to heal others and themselves.

...

The next story is about a very interesting man in Mexico, whom I had the opportunity to meet in my early adult years. He is believed to do extraordinary healing with energy.

Reflection Time:

Have you ever had a chance to experience a healing treatment with energy healing technologies?

If so, what was the outcome in your particular situation? Did you use it complimentary to conventional treatments or on its own?

If you have not tried them, would you be more open to them now?

The Miracle That Healed Jesus

Indigenous roots and belief systems are the bases of what makes Mexican culture so rich.

The tapestries of colors aren't just seen in hand-woven textiles, pretty pottery, jewelry, humor, storytelling, history, food and architecture, but in the people, our belief systems, our connection to the spirit realms, nature and natural medicine.

I was visiting Grandma Minnie's house the summer I broke things off with my high school boyfriend, Ralph.

Grandma Minnie's powerful healing energy healed my body, heart, mind and soul.

However, spending time at her house meant spending time with uncle Jose and uncle Juan, two of my dad's brothers.

Their battles with drug addiction and alcohol were tough to beat. Addictions are complicated, with deep roots.

When my siblings and I were little, my uncles would take us to a nearby park in their VW Beetle.

Beatles' songs would play in the background, "Yellow Submarine," "I Get High with A Little Help from My Friends," or "Lucy in The Sky with Diamonds."

On the way to the park, they'd light up a joint and be flying high by the time we got to the park.

Back in the 70s, the idea of second-hand smoke and its effects on health wasn't of concern, and let's just say that common sense didn't really enter the minds of two young men with addictive personalities.

Many times, I saw syringes, spoons and a dark liquid residue on their night stands because they'd gotten so high that they'd forget to put away their paraphernalia.

Part of the reason I stayed away from drugs and alcohol for most of my life was because I witnessed the effects drugs had on their lives: their behavior, suffering, resistance to accepting responsibility, and the deterioration of their relationships.

Been there, seen it, done it (second hand), at the age of three. So passé.

It was also the reason I wouldn't date anyone with addictions, no matter what the addiction was.

Unfortunately, for uncle Juan, sex, drugs and rock n' roll caught up with him. He was diagnosed with cirrhosis of the liver and given a very short prognosis.

I knew my favorite uncle, Jose, was sick. No one had to tell me. It was pretty obvious, but no one in the family was willing to talk openly about HIV. They just hoped for the best. Mexican culture doesn't promote airing dirty laundry.

He lived at Grandma Minnie's home till he passed in the year 2000 from complications.

Uncle Juan lived at Grandma Minnie's in between marriages. He was married at the time to wife number two, Catherine, a German national.

She lived with him and their two daughters in a house that Grandma Minnie bought for them in Cuernavaca, the city of eternal Spring, with steady temperatures all year at approximately 25 degrees Celsius.

Juan was a brilliant talker and charmer, but had a hard time keeping jobs.

Grandma Minnie and I were invited to visit them in Cuernavaca one weekend.

We took a bus from the nearby bus terminal and arrived about an hour later.

It was my first ever experience travelling on a bus full of boxes with chickens and live animals; something that I'd only ever seen in the movies.

To my surprise, it was a real occurrence and an experience I was grateful for.

When we arrived at the bus terminal in Cuernavaca, I was sad to say 'good-bye' to the chicks and hens that had kept us company.

Uncle Juan was waiting for us on the main platform. He grabbed our overnight bags and placed them in his car.

"We're going to see Chak this evening. Would you like to come with us?" he asked when we were on our way to their house.

"Chak?" I asked with a chuckle.

"Yes. There is a man who channels his spirit. When he does, he heals people, and sometimes does operations on people. But we cannot say a word. It's all very clandestine."

I raised an eyebrow. "What do you mean, does operations? Like, he opens people up?"

"Yes."

"Is he a doctor?"

"No."

"So, how does he know what to do?"

"The spirit of Chak takes over his body and does the healing. He healed our friend Jesús, and hundreds of others, including government officials and politicians. But it's all very hush-hush."

"OK," I said with trepidation, "So, what does this guy do for a living when he's not being a surgeon?"

"He's a mechanic."

"Like, a car mechanic?"

"Yes. The work he does is real," Uncle Juan clarified. "I've seen it with my own eyes."

"You've seen the surgeries?"

"Yes."

"Don't people bleed out?"

"No."

"How does that happen?"

"I don't know, but people don't bleed out."

"Interesting."

When we got to my aunt and uncle's, we had dinner, then waited until sundown to drive to the secret location, which my aunt and uncle knew well.

The clandestine clinics were moved every week among their group of friends. The location was disclosed last minute to avoid raising attention from non-believers, negative people, and most importantly, the authorities.

We arrived at a beautiful large home.

My aunt and uncle knew the owners well. They greeted each other and introduced Grandma Minnie and me.

We were shown to a hallway that led to a bedroom at the far end of the house.

Then we were asked to stand at the front of a 'waiting' line just outside the bedroom.

Both my aunt and uncle volunteered at the events, so they were considered members of the 'community.'

"Wait here," the host said.

We waited for about thirty minutes until the person ahead of my uncle came out of the room.

They seemed a bit groggy.

Another volunteer led the person down the hallway and out of the house.

It was my uncle's turn to go in.

I peeked my head into the room. There was a single bed against a wall, and the man they referred to as Chak sat on a chair beside the bed.

He had dark hair, brown skin, a round face and a heavy constitution.

Uncle Juan was instructed to lie down on the bed. I had to step out of the room and wait with my grandmother until his session was over.

Aunt Catherine was busy helping in other areas of the house.

The entire operation was run with the utmost precision, like a Swiss clock.

My uncle emerged from the room about an hour later.

He walked slowly.

We helped him down the stairs, and then Aunt Catherine drove home.

Once we were in the car, I couldn't keep my curiosity at bay any longer. "What happened?"

"He gave me a new liver," Uncle Juan said.

"He actually cut you open?" I asked.

"Yes."

"How did he give you a new liver?"

"He regenerates the organs."

"Like out of thin air?"

"Yes."

"OK," I said with a deep sense of doubt, "Now what?"

"I'm supposed to rest for two weeks and let my body heal. This is no different than a regular surgery. I'm also supposed to drink the teas made from the herbs that he prescribed."

"OK," I said, but wanted to know more.

He continued, "Then I'm supposed to ask my doctors for another ultrasound."

I had no idea why he'd instruct him to do that, but soon learned why.

"He said this is the last opportunity I'm being given. I have to stop drinking or he will not give me a new liver again."

I knew that was going to be his biggest challenge.

The next day, my grandmother and I took a bus back to Mexico City and waited to hear back with regards to the ultrasound.

My grandmother had high hopes.

Two weeks passed. The phone rang. My grandmother picked up the call.

It was my uncle.

My grandmother's face suddenly lit up like a Christmas tree as she paid close attention to his words, "My liver is 100% healthy. The doctors cannot explain it. They asked if I'd had a transplant done."

I almost fell of my chair when she told me.

She turned to me, "Don't you ever question God's power!"

I had no smart-ass comments to make. It took me a moment to regain my composure.

Uncle Juan was lucky. He never had issues with his liver again.

However, he didn't stop drinking, and his life spiraled into a black hole. His wife divorced him and went back to Germany with their daughters.

He didn't contest her decision as long as he didn't have to pay child support.

Unfortunately, not all stories have happy endings. People's choices will take them down different paths. Ultimately, the choice is unique to each of us, as well as the outcome.

…

This story is the reason I needed to bring up the subject of limiting beliefs in the chapter ahead.

Reflection Time:

Have you ever experienced a miraculous healing event that happened in your body or to someone close to you?

If so, how did it affect your life and belief systems?

If not, did this story spark curiosity in you about the possibility of healing with energy?

The Power of Limiting Beliefs

Beliefs, thoughts, and emotions are energy, and our belief systems affect the way in which we see the world, as well as how we experience our potential.

Whenever my sister Monica called me "stupid," which was often, my mom always corrected her by saying, "Don't say that. Everyone has the same potential, but not everyone is able to reach it."

I'm not sure if that was meant as a compliment, but let's put that aside for now...

Everyone has limiting beliefs.

If you believe that you're not smart enough to achieve things, you won't.

In the same way, if you believe that you can achieve anything in life, you will.

Our thoughts and focus create our reality.

This is why competitive athletes are taught to visualize victory prior to competitions. That is, of course, if they are fortunate enough to work with coaches who understand the power of the mind.

When we're kids, our belief systems are programmed into our unconscious mind by our parents and the people around us.

Often, children learn not to question authority, which is something that really bothers me.

Instead of encouraging kids to think for themselves, and use logical and intuitive decision-making skills, they're often taught to accept what is being presented or dictated to them.

To a degree, children need guidance, but I believe that they'll be more confident children if they're empowered to make their own decisions, and that their voice matters.

From childhood, they move into their teenage years, where if they're lucky, they'll be allowed to rebel and question authority figures.

Otherwise, they'll develop into adults that are easily mislead and manipulated by what they watch on the news and by other people's opinions.

The same thing happens when people learn to develop their intuition.

I was fortunate that no one taught me how to talk to souls. It just happened.

I've met many psychics and mediums, who gave me information that I now know was true for them, but not necessarily for me.

It is my belief that each person's truth is just that, and therefore, everyone is right when it comes to convictions.

Your beliefs become your reality.

Therefore, if you believe that in order to speak to spirits, you must do a headstand and say ten Hail Mary's, then that's how you'll connect.

If you believe that it's impossible to speak to spirits, then that will be your truth.

See where I'm going with this?

Everyone is right because it is what you believe that makes things a reality.

There is nothing cast in stone, so all of it is correct, as long as you wish to believe it.

There are also a multitude of ways to arrive at the same result.

Our thoughts are energy, our beliefs are energy, our emotions, words, actions, all of it…and energy is malleable, so what you believe about the past, present, or future becomes your reality.

This is why you can have three siblings live through the exact same trauma and have completely different perspectives of, and effects from that same event.

Hence the reason why Alfred Hitchcock's movies were so brilliant.

Many experts who teach courses on how to develop intuitive abilities, teach what they learned from others or from their own personal experience through their own filter.

No one bothers to question what they learn. The students take it, own it, make it theirs and continue passing it on.

This is no different than people who learn to cook spaghetti a certain way from their mother, who learned from her mother and so forth. They all cook it the way they do because that's how their mother did it. But no one ever thinks to ask their mother why, or if they do, the answer is often, "because that's how my mother taught me."

As Master Yoda said in the movie, *The Empire Strikes Back*, "You must unlearn what you have learned."

What I've found most useful in my development as a person, writer, facilitator, medium and psychic, is not to let other people's limiting beliefs affect my possibilities.

Life is full of infinite possibilities, so don't get bogged down by what you hear or learn from others. Give yourself permission to explore.

Respect different beliefs, but develop your own by allowing yourself to step into your own possibilities.

This is especially important when you're manifesting, and more so when manifesting abundance.

…

We've talked limiting beliefs, but now let's talk about the most powerful energy that exists, which just happens to be an emotion: love.

Reflection Time:

Let's face it. Everyone has limiting beliefs.

What are some of the limiting beliefs that creep in on you with regards to your own spirituality?

What are some of the ways that you've tried to deal with them, if any?

How do you believe you'll look at your limiting beliefs and those of others from now on?

The Miracle of Self-Love

The year 2015 was not a great year for me in many ways. To say that it was filled with life lessons I wasn't particularly fond of, is an understatement.

My father and step-mother had been taking turns going in and out of the emergency room at the local hospital every month over the previous four years.

I'd also experienced the loss of a pregnancy in 2013.

In 2014, one of my best friends, Len, passed away suddenly from an aortic aneurysm.

Len was the poster child for 'nice' guy. He was like the older brother I never had. Losing him was devastating.

The night I found out, I sobbed in bed in a fetal position.

Suddenly, I felt him lie behind me in a spooning position, putting his arm around me and saying, "Everything is going to be OK."

"How? You're here in spirit, but you're not *here*!"

"Gab, you know all the shit you used to say to us when I was alive about God and spirits, that God is omnipresent and omnipowerful, and I used to think you were crazy?"

"Yeah."

"Well, it's all true. You were right!"

"I know that, but it doesn't make it any easier. You left four kids and a wife. Shouldn't you be with them?"

"I am."

"No, you're with me."

"I'm with them and you at the same time. I'm telling you, Mexicana, all the shit you used to talk about is true! When I'm here, I'm there too. I don't have to split myself or separate myself. I'm fully present with everyone at the same time."

That gave me comfort, but I still felt a great deal of grief.

Although I considered myself to have above average strength and character, I'd reached a low point in my life.

I'd given up everything in life to 'help take care' of my ill father at the request of my stepmother.

I gave up my business, car, luxury condo by the water in Toronto, and basically the life I knew.

I was single, so I figured it was the right thing to do, and it would give me the opportunity to get to know my father better before he died.

But everything that could have gone wrong, went wrong.

I felt more alone than I ever had. For the first time in my life, I experienced depression, something I hadn't been willing to become familiar with, but it creeped up and hit me like a truck.

Looking back now, I realize I was going through perimenopause, which leads to an upheaval of emotions like a volcano erupting, due to the hormonal changes in the body and repressed emotions from the past.

This was further complicated by an underlying autoimmune condition that affected my entire endocrine system, including my thyroid, and the domino effect on my body hit me like a hurricane.

I had tremors, which meant I couldn't sign anything or feed myself at times. The chronic fatigue and insomnia knocked me down, but I fought back. I'd walk my dog for 15 minutes and then nap for two hours to recover. I slept on and off for 16 hours per day.

I was irritable and emotionally irrational. I experienced bouts of anxiety and panic attacks. My memory was failing. I couldn't even remember my friends' names, which was embarrassing. I had tachycardia, which felt like my heart would pop out of my body at any moment.

I gained weight instead of losing it, which was a rare symptom with that particular condition, but possible.

My reproductive system was completely out of control and as a result, I hemorrhaged two liters of blood every month.

I realized the Universe had been encouraging me to go back to Canada for good and focus on my life and health rather than sacrificing myself for others.

I was lucky enough to have a friend who offered me his home while I got back on my feet.

I thanked Source.

When I told another friend that I could not believe just how lucky I was to have friends who literally stepped over each other to offer their help to me, she said, "Are you serious? You don't know?"

"No," I said.

"Gaby, your friends are a reflection of you."

I sighed and reflected on her words for a moment.

"I hadn't thought of it that way."

"Let your friends be there for you the way you're always there for everyone when they need you."

Then I remembered what my friend Len had said to me years earlier, when I tried to pay for his time because he came over to my condo to fix a leaky faucet.

"Mexicana! Why don't you ever let people help you? Your friends care about you. You're a single woman, on your own. Let us help you! Put that money away!"

I felt so blessed, and thanked the Universe once again.

I was tired of feeling defeated, so I chose to step into my power and manifested, "Universe, I know I could be manifesting a home, car, and more, but right now, the only focus is my health, so please guide me in the right direction, and help me find the people who will help me heal."

I began treatment immediately with allopathic medicine to bring my heartbeat to normal levels.

Then, a friend referred me to a Heilkunst homeopathic practitioner and I learned that classical homeopaths go through four years of intense training, while Heilkunst homeopaths go through eight years of training and deal with complicated conditions like mine.

Ellie, the Heilkunst practitioner, used tough love. "You either do as I say or don't waste my time or your money."

I had nothing to lose. "I'll do whatever you tell me to do."

What I loved about working with her was that she never told me to stop taking allopathic medicine.

"On the contrary, it will just work faster, more effectively," she said.

I respected and appreciated that approach.

I also sought the help of a naturopathic doctor-in-training at the College of Naturopathic Medicine in Toronto because at the time, I couldn't afford to pay the rates of private naturopaths.

The last part of the puzzle was my commitment to learning how to love myself unconditionally.

I had always told myself that I loved myself, but in retrospect, I realized that my idea of self-love was very conditional.

Every day, I looked in the mirror and said, "I love you."

The first time I did it, I thought it was the most ridiculous thing I'd ever done.

Of course, I loved myself!

The second time I did it, I cried uncontrollably because I realized that I'd been lying to myself all along. My 'self-love' was conditional and it was time to change that.

I started hugging myself, but it wasn't easy to give myself the love and care I needed. I was so used to giving it out vs. receiving it.

So, I had to pretend to be my own daughter and imagine all the things I'd want to say to her, do for her to empower her, guide her.

The experience was surreal, but necessary. That's how resistant I was to turning love inwards.

That lesson was one of my biggest lessons, and I was so grateful for it. I had to be broken in order to rebuild myself the best way possible.

In the process of going through all the layers of my trauma with my Heilkunst practitioner, she explained to me that autoimmune conditions develop when a person sacrifices for others without regard for self.

Gulp!

Self-sacrifice had been my modus operandi my entire life.

As I went through my healing journey on a mental, emotional, physical and energetic level, I realized that self-sacrifice serves no one, not even the person you're trying to help, because self-sacrifice comes from a place of 'rescuing others.'

Also, there is a huge difference between helping and rescuing. Helping facilitates the person to step into their power. Whereas rescuing takes their power away and no one likes to have their power taken away.

This isn't to say that we never need to be there for others. There are times, like caring for children and elderly parents, that we don't have a choice, but jumping at the first opportunity to rescue doesn't serve us or the people whom we think need help, even without having asked for help.

When we turn our attention and focus onto others, we're avoiding focus and attention on our own work.

I pretended to be my own daughter until I felt comfortable enough to be me, loving myself.

It took a few months, but I got to a point in my healing journey when I looked at myself naked in front of a mirror, grabbed the fat on my belly and said, "I love you even with this extra fat. There's more of you to love."

I meant it and knew I was on the right track to becoming authentically me.

I had never been able to say, "I love you" to myself when I had the 'perfect' body in my younger years.

This was growth.

Before seeing the naturopathic doctor and his intern for the first time, I went to the health food store to buy some of the supplements I had a feeling I'd need in order to complement my healing.

I stood in front of a wall of supplements, not really sure what to grab.

Then I heard my friend Len say, "Take this, and that…" and he guided me to all the vitamins I should buy.

I went home with a bag full of vitamins and started taking them right away, even though I wasn't sure if I was taking the right doses.

When I met with the naturopath at the College and he asked about the supplements I was taking, I showed him the list from A to Z.

"How did you know that these are exactly the supplements you should be on?"

I wanted more than anything to say that the spirit of my dead friend Len told me what to buy, but I had to be careful not to give anyone cause to send me for psychiatric assessment.

Instead, I said another truth, "I grew up with natural medicine my whole life, so I kind of know what I'm doing."

"This is amazing! The only thing I would change is the dose on two of these, but otherwise, you're on exactly the supplements that are indicated for this condition."

I felt a huge sense of relief and validation.

I began to notice, though, that the approach to naturopathic medicine is based on the same philosophy as that of allopathic medicine, which is to treat symptoms, not the root cause of dysfunction. Regardless, I knew it would be a great complement to my healing.

On a follow-up visit, the naturopathic intern I was seeing at the college suggested we change my diet to an immune suppressant diet, but Len immediately interjected, "Tell her she's incorrect. What you need to do is bring up your immune system as high as it will go, so it can reset itself and start working properly."

"That makes no sense at all," she said.

"Well, I'm not going to follow your diet," I said.

I trusted Len beyond a doubt.

The allopathic specialist I was seeing, an endocrinologist, wasn't open to natural medicine, but I wanted him to be aware of everything I was doing, so I confessed.

He wasn't pleased, but knew he couldn't force me to get off the supplements.

Within three months, I was off the allopathic medication that was treating my heart palpitations.

The specialist said, "I'm so happy for you. You no longer need medication, which is great because most people end up having to take radioactive iodine."

"I told you that this disease wasn't going to be around long, Doctor," I said.

"Yes, but I hope you don't think this had anything to do with all the natural mumbo-jumbo that you believe in."

"Of course not," I said.

He'd never seen a case improve so quickly, but my natural approach had nothing to do with it.... sure.

The homeopathic process took longer than the other two therapies because energetically, I had to 'clear' all the emotions and traumatic events on my timeline that had contributed to me getting sick in the first place.

I had nine pages of traumatic events on my timeline. We would go through each, once per month.

On our initial consultation, I said, "I guess I'll be with you for the rest of my life, but at least I'll die healthy." We both laughed.

Within six months, I was officially in remission.

Two and a half years later, the endocrinologist ran the last tests that showed I was still in remission. He couldn't hide his surprise.

"I know you said it sometimes comes back, but I told you it wouldn't," I said.

"I know you did, but I can't believe it. What we usually see is people having their thyroids removed. I'm so happy for you."

The physical recovery took a while longer.

I worked with a physiotherapist to get my muscles back to normal strength because through the entire ordeal, my muscles weakened.

Lack of motion is one of the worst things you can do to a human body, and sixteen hours of sleep per day took a toll on mine.

I also gained an appreciation for the weight I put on. In rare cases of that specific type of thyroid dysfunction, weight gain rather than loss, can happen. However, if I'd lost 35 lbs. while starting at 125 lbs., I would have ended up weighing below 90 lbs., which could have complicated matters for me, and likely killed me.

I truly believe that the weight gain saved my life.

On the plus side, I learned to appreciate the healing benefits of rest and sleep. Before I got sick, I used to dislike sleeping more than seven hours per night, but afterwards, I really enjoyed sleeping nine to ten hours.

Through the process of learning to love myself, I gave myself permission to be OK with doing nothing.

My busy type A personality could take a rest. It no longer had to be in 'production' mode at all times.

I learned to be kind and compassionate with myself, and to put myself first. I started to ask myself before giving, "Have I taken care of me first today? Do I have it in me to give authentically or would I be sacrificing me or part of me?" and "Would this person do the same for me if the roles were reversed?"

If the answer was no, I would stop.

The tendency to sacrifice ourselves for others isn't an act of kindness, but rather, lack of respect, disregard for ourselves and our wellbeing.

It's what I refer to as the 'Superhero Syndrome'', which derives from past pain and trauma, abandonment, and lack of love in our childhood.

Again, this has nothing to do with looking after our children or elderly parents.

When we give too much of ourselves, it is an unconscious way of asking to be loved and accepted more. We become people pleasers.

I stopped being a people pleaser through this journey.

Months after my endocrine specialist gave me the all clear, Len said, "Gab, I have to go."

"What do you mean, you have to go?"

"I have to go," and with that, I felt Len's spirit leave.

This isn't to say that he actually left. Spirit, after all, is omnipresent.

However, I wasn't able to feel his presence as strongly, or all the time.

I could still tune into him with intention and communicate with him, but it was with a different intensity.

The best way I can describe it, is that it was as if I had to call him on the phone, rather than talking to him anytime, anywhere because he was next to me.

I understood at that moment that he was ready to reincarnate.

The 'intensity' of his cell phone signal wouldn't be as strong as it was before, if you will.

His work with me was complete.

The idea of omnipresence, death and incarnation was explained to me through a dream.

I was told to use a carton of eggs and a scarf to demonstrate the concept to clients.

Spirit, Source or our energetic body is like a sheath (the scarf). We are all part of that sheath.

When we choose to incarnate into a body or 'sleeve,' part of that scarf goes into the egg carton, but it is always attached to the rest of the sheath and everything is part of that sheath, including the sleeves of people, animals and plants.

When we die, we leave the sleeve behind to be recycled into Mother Earth (because energy cannot be destroyed, only transformed into another type of energy).

Another fantastic metaphor or example is when a person loses a limb through amputation, they often experience what's referred to as phantom pain.

Phantom symptoms can be itching in a missing limb or the urge to go pee when there are no kidneys.

Healthcare professionals often explain the phenomena as a result of the nerve endings at the amputation site being active.

However, from the energetic perspective, when a limb or organ is missing physically, the energetic limb or organ remains. It's the same thing when the entire physical body is no longer there, the energetic body is.

The idea of separation is only a belief. It doesn't exist. The idea of not belonging is a concept. We are ONE. We cannot *not* belong.

It's our awareness that changes, but not the energetic connection, because energetically, we are all ONE. We are always connected to Source energy. When we feel disconnected, it's really our perception or awareness of the connection that has changed, not the connection itself.

When we choose the incarnation experience, we go into it much like a virtual reality game.

We put on the goggles and gloves, we go through the game and learn the lessons we came to experience. It is our mission to live the game to the fullest and give ourselves permission to do so.

Along the way, we're meant to remember all the skills we brought with us from our past life experiences.

When we choose to leave the holographic game, we do, but death is just a concept. There is no such thing as death.

We choose the human experience for a reason. It is through the human experience that we can experience emotions aside from the energy of love.

We experience life through our senses, we experience the material realm: pain, suffering, joy, strength and vulnerability. The light and the shadow side of humanity.

It is very different from the spiritual experience.

Hence, while we are in the human experience, we are meant to live to the highest experience rather than coasting through life. Coasting doesn't serve us.

The first time my friend Len asked me to turn up the song "Africa," by Toto that was playing on the radio, I asked him, "Can't you just listen to the song anytime you want now that you're dead?"

"Of course, but listening to it from your experience is different. The human experience is different. I can tune into the songs in a different way through you. I live vicariously through your experience."

"Oh!" I was fascinated by this.

"There's a reason why we choose the human experience. It rocks in its own way, as does the essence of our spirit."

This is the reason I explain to clients that living in 3D (material realm) has its benefits and drawbacks.

When people aim to ascend, or develop themselves spiritually, going through all the dimensions towards the 5D (spiritual realm) and higher, they think it's like a competition in which they'll collect points along the way.

But that's not it at all.

Spiritual ascension is simply about awareness, remembering that you can navigate between 3D and higher levels of consciousness and back.

One day you may want to be more aware of the material realm, whereas other days, you may want to be more into the spiritual realm.

It is not about staying in 4D or 5D or higher because if that was the purpose, you would never have chosen to reincarnate.

Being human gives you a different perspective.

The goal is to live your life fearlessly with authenticity, as you remember what you came here to do, a.k.a. your mission.

You are also meant to recall what you brought with you from your past life experiences, and try to achieve it all while being aware that you're fully connected to your Source energy, and that you are Source energy.

When I recovered from the autoimmune condition, I asked Source, "Why?" and the answer came by way of a social media feed, "When we place ourselves in situations where we are void of love, it is so we may learn to love ourselves."

Boom!

...

I often speak of the concept of universal connection between everyone in physical and spirit form. The next, and final chapter is a reminder of the connection we have with Source energy and hence with others.

Reflection Time:

Have you ever asked Source "why" or "why not" in relation to an event that happened in your life, and received the answer?

If so, how did you receive the answer? Did you understand the reason? What did you learn from it?

The Miracle of Connection

Through our spiritual development, we're able to become aware of the connection that exists between all of us, such as the time when I treated a client who'd never experienced Reiki before.

"I've heard so much about Reiki and want to know what it's like," she said.

"Well, it's different for everyone. I don't want to tell you what to expect during a treatment. I'd rather let you go through it and then we can talk about your experience afterwards. Is that, OK?" I asked.

"Yes," she smiled.

"The only thing I ask is that you close your eyes, relax and trust the process. I'll let you know when the treatment is complete."

"OK."

I scanned her body slowly, identified where there were some energetic blockages and balanced her chakras, one chakra at a time.

I often get visions or pick up on information about the client as I'm working on them, but I try as much as possible not to say anything until I've completed the treatment, so the client can relax and I can focus.

With this particular client, I saw an image of a tree of life, very similar, if not identical, to the tree in the movie *Avatar* .

It was bright, luminescent, massive in height and width, and absolutely beautiful.

I smiled at this vision because it evoked such feelings of peace and unconditional love throughout my body that I couldn't help but feel grateful.

I completed the treatment. "You may open your eyes now," I said.

The client took her time opening her eyes. "That was the most incredible experience ever!"

"How so?"

"I had a vision of a tree, the most beautiful tree I've ever seen!"

I smiled, "Like the tree in Avatar?"

"Yes! That's exactly what I saw! What does it mean?"

"Well, first of all, I have to tell you that I had the same vision."

"You did?"

"Yes, and to me, it's a reminder that we're all connected. It doesn't matter what we believe that connection to be. For some it's energy, for others it's God, for others it may be Mother Earth, but the connection is undeniable. The fact that we just had the same vision is proof of that connection. I never set the intention to have this connectedness with a client. It just happens naturally."

"This is blowing my mind! I never expected Reiki to be anything like this! I feel so relaxed and refreshed, like a totally different person. And to top it off, we shared the same vision!"

"Reiki, and energy in general, is magical. Energy is very real and very powerful."

"Thank you, thank you, thank you!" she said.

I thanked Source for the continued validation that we are all connected in very special ways.

...

Reflection Time:

Have you ever experienced an unexplainable connection to a person or place?

If so, what was that experience like? How did it feel?

When you think of it now, do you understand just how connected we are, even though we're not always conscious of it?

Would knowing this make you less or more judgmental towards others and yourself?

Does this help you understand a little more clearly that it is not that we lose connection to Source or our loved ones in spirit form, but our awareness of it?

What can you do on a daily basis to ensure that you are always aware of your connection to Source?

Closing Remarks

Every story I've shared with you has been about my own personal experiences, but there are many others who have had similar or even more unusual experiences in their lives, including you.

You are a walking miracle. You are the way you are for a reason. Start believing it.

The signs are all around you. All you have to do is pay attention.

So put the phone down, stop watching TV, detach from all the distractions and go inward, meditate. Spend time alone, become your own best friend. Tune into that amazing energy within. Focus on the miracle that you are and the miracles that you are part of every single day.

I used to worry when things weren't going great in my life, but I've come to recognize challenging periods as indications that I'm going to the next level.

I love using the phrase, "Rise above." This is a constant reminder not to entangle, to detach from my external environment and focus on a view from above, from Source energy.

Instead of wondering about what the outcome will be in any given situation or why things are happening the way they are (or not), I just say to myself *I'm going to the next step in my development.* Then I surrender to Divine guidance and timing by saying, *"OK. Show me the way."*

Surrender is the 'key' word here.

I realize it takes blind trust, but life and experience have taught me that I'm safe.

I hope that from this day forward, you'll begin to recognize how Source loves and guides you.

Trust that the change, shift, loss or whatever you may be going through is part of the process, even if you don't love the way the lesson is being delivered.

Remember that *you are SOURCE ENERGY, you are a MIRACLE* and that *SOURCE ENERGY IS LOVE.* Therefore, *you are LOVE.* You cannot be disconnected from Source. It is only our awareness of the connection that changes, but not the connection.

If you've searched for love your whole life, know that everything you're looking for is already inside of you. Set the intention to open yourself to receive it and you'll start experiencing *magic*.

Thank you for going on this journey with me. May your life be blessed with the awareness of the miracles that happen in your life every day, so you may *believe*.

Before I go, I have one more question for you, "What did you learn in this process?"

About the Author

Gaby Pineda is a psychic medium and medical intuitive.

She is also an empowerment, manifestation and intuition coach, Reiki Master and teacher, certified in conversational hypnosis and rapid brain recoding.

Often referred to as a "Healer for the Soul" and a "Messenger from God," Gaby's life has been touched by a series of miraculous events from the time she was conceived, right up to present day.

Gaby's mission is to empower her clients to live their authentic life fearlessly.

She is the author of several books, including *The Dating Adventures of My Traveling Panties*, about her dating misadventures, which she published under the pseudonym of E.Riley in 2011, and *Believe–A Life Touched by Miracles*, based on the miraculous experiences in her life.

Her next book, *Eulogy of a Superhero-A Story of Forgiveness and Empowerment*, is based on her life story.

For more information, visit www.gabypineda.ca.